D1331907

Contents

In this book . . .

. . . identify your child's unique character

. . . common misconceptions

. . . developing a healthy bond

. . . understanding how a child feels

. . . conveying love

. . . giving and receiving attention

. . . rewards and punishment

. . . sharing your spiritual life

. . . and more

How To Really Love Your Child

Ross Campbell

Authentic

This edition published 2006 by Authentic Media
9 Holdom Avenue, Bletchley, Milton Keynes, Bucks., MK1 1QR, UK

Authentic Media is a division of Send The Light Ltd., a company
limited by guarantee (registered charity no. 270162)

British Library Cataloguing in Publication Data
A catalogue record for this book is available from the British Library
ISBN 1-85078-675-5

Cover Design by Sam Redwood
Print Management by Adare Carwin
Printed in Great Britain by J.H. Haynes & Co., Sparkford

Foreword

This is a penetrating book, but bringing up children the right way in today's world is no light matter. This book gets down to the real issues of being a parent.

Parents haven't been trained to be parents, and so bringing up children tends to be something done rather haphazardly. Even 'successes' seem to happen accidentally. This book will guide parents in the right directions for today's lifestyles.

The author, Dr Ross Campbell, points to different areas where children will know real love; especially through eye contact, physical touch, and 'focused attention'. He reminds us of the question 'Do you love me?' that children seem to be constantly asking in their different behaviour patterns. He writes sensitively of what discipline is and its place in the home. And all of his writing is set within a Christian framework – not one that just gives pat answers but one that is determined to find a realistic way of enjoying a deeper relationship with our children.

What appealed to us especially was the author's honesty in sharing not only sound principles but also his honesty in relating how these have worked in his own family life. He doesn't shirk the problems but offers some ways out, at the same time giving us instances of both his failures and successes. The thrust of the book is not to condemn us where we have failed, but to point the better ways. What comes through strongly is the joy as well as the responsibilities of being a parent.

Dr Campbell writes as a psychiatrist but his style avoids jargon and is down to earth. We would recommend that you read this book before your children are teenagers. It's a practical book which you will want to read and re-read as you go through the teenage years with your children.

ROY AND FIONA CASTLE

Preface

T his book is for parents of children younger than adolescents. Its intention is to give mothers and fathers an understandable and practical way of approaching their wonderful, yet awesome, task of raising each child. My concerns are the needs of children and how best to meet them.

This whole area of child rearing is in itself a complex venture with which most parents today are having great difficulty. Unfortunately, the outpouring of books, articles, lectures, and seminars regarding children have largely frustrated and bewildered parents despite the fact much of the information has been excellent.

I believe the problem has been that many books, articles, and lectures have homed in on one, or at most, only a few specific aspects of child rearing without covering the subject fully, or without clearly defining the specific area they are covering. Consequently, many conscientious parents have earnestly attempted to apply what they have read or heard as the fundamental way of relating to a child, and often fail. Their failure is not usually due to error in the information read or heard, nor in the way it is applied.

The problem, as I see it, usually lies in the parents not having a general, balanced perspective on how to relate to a child. Most parents have the essential information *per se*, but there is confusion about *when* to apply *which* principle under *what* circumstance. This confusion is understandable. Parents have been told what to do, but not when to do it, nor, in many cases, how to do it.

The classic example of this is in the area of discipline. Excellent books and seminars on childhood have addressed the issue of discipline but failed to make clear that discipline is only one way of relating to a child. Many parents, consequently, conclude that discipline is the basic and primary way of treating a child. This is an easy mistake to make especially when one hears the statement, 'If you love your child, you must discipline your child.' This statement is, of course, true, but the tragedy is that many parents discipline almost *totally* while showing little love which can be felt or bring comfort to a child. Hence, most children doubt that they are genuinely, unconditionally loved. So again, the problem is not whether to discipline; the problem is how to manifest our love to a child through discipline and when to show it in other, more affectionate, ways.

I address these problems in a plain, understandable way, in order to demonstrate how to *generally* approach child rearing. In addition, I hope to provide information which will help parents determine the correct action for each situation. Of course, handling every circumstance correctly is impossible; however, the closer we come to this, the better parents we become, the more gratified we are, and the happier our child becomes.

Much of the material in this book has come from lecture series that I have given over past years at numerous conferences on parent-child relationships.

1

The problem

'**A**s Tommy was growing up, he was such a good boy, so well behaved,' Esther Smith, her husband, Jim, at her side, began as the grieving parents unfolded their painful story in my counselling room. 'Yes, he seemed content and never gave us much trouble. We made sure he had the right experiences – scouts, baseball, church and all. Now he is fourteen and is forever fighting with his brother and sister – but that's just sibling rivalry, isn't it? Other than that, Tom – he's no longer Tommy – has never been a real problem for us,' Esther Smith concluded. 'He is moody sometimes and goes to his room for long periods. But he has never been disrespectful or disobeyed or back-talked. His father saw to that.

'There's one thing we *know* he has gotten plenty of and that's discipline. In fact, that's the most puzzling thing of all. How can a child so well disciplined all his life suddenly begin running around with undisciplined peers and do the things they do? And show such disrespect for his parents and other adults? These children even lie, steal, and drink alcohol. I can't trust Tom anymore. I can't talk with him. He's so sullen and quiet. He won't even look at me. He doesn't seem to want anything to do with us. And he's doing so poorly in school this year.'

'When did you notice these changes in Tom?' I asked.

Jim Smith looked up at the ceiling. 'Let me think. He's fourteen now, almost fifteen', he said. 'His grades were the first problem we noticed. About two years ago. During the last few months of sixth grade, we noticed he became bored first with school, then with other things. He began to hate going to church. Later Tom even lost interest in his friends and spent more and more time by himself, usually in his room. He talked less and less.

'But things really worsened when he began junior high school. Tom lost interest in his favourite activities – even sports. That's when he completely dropped his old stand-by friends and began running around with boys who were usually in trouble. Tom's attitude changed and conformed to theirs. He placed little value in grades and wouldn't study. These friends of his often got him in trouble.'

'And we've tried everything.' Mrs Smith took up the account. 'First we spanked him. Then we took away privileges like television, movies, and so on. One time we grounded him for a solid month. We've tried to reward him for appropriate behaviour. I really believe we have tried every recommendation we have heard or read. I really wonder if anyone can help us or help Tom.'

'What did we do wrong? Are we bad parents? God knows we've tried hard enough,' Jim Smith added. 'Maybe it's congenital. Maybe it's something Tom inherited. Could it be physical? But our pediatrician examined him a couple of weeks ago. Should we take him to a gland specialist? Should we get an EEG? We need help. Tom needs help. We love our boy, Dr Campbell. What can we do to help him? Something's got to be done.'

Later, after Mr and Mrs Smith departed, Tom entered the counselling room. I was impressed with his naturally likable ways and handsome appearance. However, his gaze was downcast and when he would make eye contact, it was only for a moment. Although obviously a bright child, Tom spoke only in short, gruff phrases and grunts. Finally, when he felt comfortable enough to share his story, he revealed essentially the same factual material as his parents. Going further, he said, 'No one really cares about me except my friends.'

'No one?' I asked.

'No. Maybe my parents. I don't know. I used to think they cared about me when I was little. I guess it doesn't matter much now anyway. All they really care about are their own friends, jobs, activities, and things.

'They don't need to know what I do, anyway. It's none of their business. I just want to be away from them and lead my own life. Why should they be so concerned about me? They never were before.'

As the conversation progressed, it became clear that Tom was quite depressed, never having times when he felt content with himself or his life. He had longed for a close, warm relationship with his parents as long as he could remember, but during the last few months he had slowly given up his dream. He turned to peers who would accept him, but his unhappiness deepened even more.

So here is a common tragic situation today. An early adolescent boy who, by all apparent indications, was doing well during his early years. Until he was around twelve or thirteen years of age, no one guessed that Tom was unhappy. During those years he was a complacent child who made few demands on his parents, teachers, or others. So none suspected he did not feel completely loved and accepted. Despite his having parents who deeply loved him and cared for him, Tom did not *feel* genuinely loved. Yes, he knew of his parents' love and concern for him and never would have told you otherwise. Nonetheless, the incomparable emotional well-being of feeling completely and unconditionally loved and accepted was not his.

This is truly difficult to understand, because Tom's parents are indeed good parents. They love him, and take care of his needs to the best of their knowledge. In raising Tom, Jim and Esther Smith have applied what they have heard and read and have sought advice from others. And their marriage is definitely above average. They do love and respect each other.

A familiar story

Most parents have a difficult time raising their children. With pressures and strains mounting every day upon the family, it is easy to become confused and discouraged. Rising divorce rates, economic crises, declining quality of education, and loss of trust in leadership all take an emotional toll of everyone. As parents become more physically, emotionally, and spiritually drained, it becomes increasingly difficult to nurture a child. I am convinced that a child takes the greatest brunt of these difficult times. A child is the most needy person in our society, and his greatest need is love.

The story of Tom Smith is familiar today. His parents do love him deeply. They have done their best in rearing him, but something is missing. Did you notice what it was? No, not love, the parents *do* love him. The basic problem is that Tom does not *feel* loved. Should the parents be blamed? Is it their fault? I don't think so. The truth is that Mr and Mrs Smith have always loved their son, but never knew how to show it. Like most parents, they believed they were meeting Tom's needs: food, shelter, clothes, education, love, guidance, etc. Yes, they met all these needs but were overlooking his need for love, unconditional love. Although love is within the heart of almost all parents, the challenge is to *convey* this love.

I believe that, despite the problems in today's living, any parents who genuinely desire to give a child what he needs, can be taught to do so. In order to give him everything they can in the short time he is with them, all parents need to know how to truly love their children.

Which form of discipline is most appropriate?

'I remember one time when I was six or seven. Even now it makes me unhappy to think about it, and sometimes it makes me mad,' Tom continued in a session with me a few days later. 'I had accidentally broken a window with a ball. I felt terrible about it and hid in the woods until Mum came looking for me. I was so sorry and I remember crying because I felt I had been very bad. When Dad came home, Mum told him about the window and he smacked me.' Tears had welled up in Tom's eyes.

I asked, 'What did you say then?'

'Nothing,' he muttered.

This incident illustrates another area of confusion in handling children, that of discipline. In this example, the way Tom was disciplined caused him to have feelings of pain, anger, and resentment towards his parents which he will never forget or forgive without help.

Now years afterward, Tom still hurt from that happening. Why did that particular incident make such an unpleasant imprint on his memory? There were other times when he accepted spankings with no problems, and on occasion was even thankful. Could it have been because he already felt sorry and repentant over his breaking the window? Had he already suffered enough for his mistake without enduring physical pain? Could the spanking have convinced Tom that his parents did not understand him as a person or were not sensitive to his feelings? Could he have needed his parents' warmth and understanding at that particular time rather than harsh punishment? If so, how could Tom's parents know? And, if so, how could they discern which form of discipline was most appropriate at that particular time?

What do you think, fellow parents? Should we decide in advance what action we will routinely take in raising a child? Do you think we should be consistent? How consistent? Should we use punishment each time our child misbehaves? If so, should it always be the same? If not, what are the alternatives? What is discipline? Are discipline and punishment synonymous? Should we study one school of thought, for example, Parent Effectiveness Training, and stick by it? Or should we use some of our own common sense and intuition? Or some of each? How much? When?

These are questions every conscientious parent is struggling with today. We are bombarded with books, articles, seminars, and institutes about how to rear our children. Approaches vary from pinching a child's trapezius muscle to the use of candy as a reward.

In short, how could the parents have handled this situation in a way that would discipline Tom and yet maintain a loving, warm relationship with him? We'll look into this difficult subject later.

I think all parents agree that rearing a child today is especially difficult. One reason is that so much of a child's time is under the control and influence of others; for instance, school, church, neighbours, and peers. Because of this many parents feel no matter how good a

job they do, their efforts have little overall effect upon
their child.

The opposite is true

Just the opposite is true. Every study I've read indicates
that the home wins hands down in every case. The influence of parents far outweighs everything else. The home
holds the upper hand in determining how happy,
secure, and stable a child is; how a child gets along with
adults, peers, and different children; how confident a
youngster is in himself and his abilities; how affectionate
he is or how aloof; how he responds to unfamiliar situations. Yes, the home, despite many distractions for a
child, has the greatest influence on him.

But the home is not the only thing that determines
what a child becomes. We should not make the mistake
of totally blaming the home for every problem or disappointment. For the sake of fairness and completeness, I
believe we must take a look at the second greatest influence upon a child.

Congenital temperament

Actually there are many congenital temperaments.
Nine have been identified to date. The research which
has given us this knowledge has been done by Dr Stella
Chess and Dr Alexander Thomas. The data have been
reported in their book. *Temperament and Behavior
Disorder in Children*, published by University Press,
New York.

This book has been acclaimed a classic and is a truly
great contribution to the world of behavioural science. It

goes a long way in explaining why children have the individual characteristics they do. It helps explain why some children are easier to raise than others. Why some children are more lovable or easier to handle. Why children raised in the same family or in very similar circumstances can be so different.

Best of all, Chess and Thomas have shown that how a child turns out is determined not only by the home environment, but also by his or her own personal traits. This has had wonderful results in alleviating much unjustified blame toward parents of children with problems. It is an unfortunate habit of many (including professionals) to assume that parents are fully to blame for everything regarding their child. The research of Chess and Thomas proves that some children are more prone to difficulties than others.

Let's look briefly at their research. Nine temperaments that can be identified in a newborn nursery have been described. These temperaments are not only congenital (present at birth) but are basic characteristics of a child that tend to stay with him. These characteristics can be modified by a child's environment; nonetheless, the temperaments are well ingrained in a child's total personality, do *not* change easily, and can persist throughout life. These nine congenital temperaments are:

1. *Activity level* is the degree of motor activity a child inherently possesses and determines how active or passive he is.
2. *Rhythmicity* (regularity versus irregularity) is the predictability of such functions as hunger, feeding pattern, elimination, and sleep-awake cycle.
3. *Approach or withdrawal* is the nature of a child's response to a new stimulus such as a new food, toy, or person.

4. *Adaptability* is the speed and ease with which a current behaviour can be modified in response to altered environmental structuring.
5. *Intensity of reaction* is the amount of energy used in mood expression.
6. *Threshold of responsiveness* is the intensity level of stimulus required to make a response.
7. *Quality of mood* (positive mood versus negative mood): playful, pleasant, joyful, friendly, as contrasted with unpleasant, crying, unfriendly behaviour.
8. *Distractability* identifies the effect of extraneous environment on direction of ongoing behaviour.
9. *Attention span and persistence* is the length of time an activity is pursued by a child and the continuation of an activity in face of obstacles.

The third, fourth, fifth, and seventh temperaments are the most crucial in determining whether a child will be easy or difficult to rear. A child with a high degree of reactivity (highly 'emotional'); a child who tends to withdraw in a new situation (a 'withdrawer'); a child who has difficulty adapting to new situations (cannot tolerate change); or a child who is usually in a bad mood – these children are quite vulnerable to stress, especially to high parental expectations. And unfortunately, they tend to receive less love and affection from adults.

The lesson to learn here is that a child's basic characteristics have much to do with the type of mothering and nurturing he or she receives.

Using these nine temperaments, Chess and Thomas assigned numerical values to evaluate newborn children. From this data they were able to predict clearly which children would be 'easy babies', that is, easy to care for, easy to relate to, and easy to raise. The children who were difficult to care for, difficult to relate to, and difficult to raise were called 'difficult babies'. They would require more from their mothers than would 'easy babies'.

Then Chess and Thomas compared how the children progress according to the type of mothering they received. Chess and Thomas studied the babies with 'nurturing' mothers (mothers who wanted their children and were able to provide a loving atmosphere where the children felt accepted). The two researchers also studied 'non-nurturing' mothers (mothers who consciously or subconsciously rejected their babies or were not able to provide an atmosphere where the children felt accepted and loved). The graph below summarises their findings.

As you can see, the 'easy' babies and 'nurturing' mothers were a great combination. These children developed well with almost no negative consequences.

The 'nurturing' mothers with 'difficult' babies had some problems with their children, but these situations were overwhelmingly positive. Overall, in the loving atmosphere provided by their mothers, these children did well.

The 'easy' babies who had 'non-nurturing' mothers generally did not do as well. They had more difficulties than the 'difficult' babies with nurturing mothers. Their experiences were somewhat more negative than positive.

Not surprisingly, the 'difficult' babies with the 'non-nurturing' mothers were most unfortunate. These children were in such difficult predicaments that they were

	Nurturing Mothers		Non-Nurturing Mothers
Easy babies	+	+	−
Difficult babies	+	−	− −

aptly called 'high-risk' children. The situations of these children is heartbreaking. They are in danger of everything imaginable from child-abuse to abandonment. They are indeed our high-risk children.

So, as we put all this invaluable material together, some extremely important facts began to emerge. First of all, how a child gets along in the world does not depend only on his home environment and parenting. The basic congenital characteristics of each child have a strong effect on how he develops, progresses, and matures.

These traits also affect and often determine how easy or difficult a child is to care for and how frustrating he might be to his parents. This, in turn, influences the parents' handling of a child. It's a two-way street.

Learning these facts has helped many guilt-ridden parents in my daily practice.

Another important lesson for parents to learn is that despite what type of congenital temperaments a child may possess, the type of mothering (and fathering, of course) is more important in determining how a child will do. Study the graph again. Although a 'difficult' child is, of course, more difficult to rear, the type of emotional nurturing has more influence in determining the final outcome. Parenting can change these congenital temperaments positively or negatively.

That's what this book is all about. It's a how-to book: how to relate to your child so he will grow to be his best; how to give your child the emotional nurturing he needs so badly. It is impossible to cover every aspect of child rearing here. I have therefore included what I feel is the most basic material for effective parenting.

It is a fact that most parents have a feeling of love toward their children and assume that they convey this love to a child. This is the greatest error today. Most parents are not transmitting their own heartfelt love to their children, and the reason is that they do not know how. Consequently, many children do not feel genuinely, unconditionally loved and accepted.

This, I believe, is true in relation to most problems that develop in children. Unless parents have a basic love-bond relationship with their children, everything else (discipline, peer relationships, school performance) is on a faulty foundation and problems will result.

This book provides the crucial basics in establishing a love-bond relationship.

2

The setting

Before we get into the basics of how to genuinely love and discipline a child, it is important to look at the prerequisites of good child rearing. The first and most important of these is the home. We will touch only a few of the essential points.

The most important relationship in the family is the marital relationship. It takes primacy over all others including the parent-child relationship. Both the quality of the parent-child bond and the child's security are largely dependent on the quality of the marital bond. So you can see why it is important to help a husband and wife to have a good relationship before attempting to solve problems they may have in child rearing. The better a marital relationship, the more effective and gratifying will be the application of later information.

However, if you are a single parent, let me assure you that what we discuss in this book applies just as much to you, dear parent. In many ways single parenting is more difficult, yet in some ways easier. But whether two parents or one, the way we relate to our children makes the difference in any home.

We can start by realising that there is a difference between cognitive (that is, intellectual or rational) communication and emotional (that is, feeling) communication. Persons who communicate primarily on a cognitive level deal mainly with factual data. They talk about such topics as sports, the stock market, money, houses, and jobs, keeping the subject of conversation out of the emotional area. Usually they are quite uncomfortable dealing with issues which elicit feelings, especially unpleasant feelings such as anger. Consequently, they avoid talking about subjects which involve love, fear, and anger. Those persons have difficulty, then, being warm and supportive of their spouses.

Others communicate more on the feeling level. They tire easily of purely factual data, and feel a need to share feelings, especially with their spouses. They feel the atmosphere between husband and wife must be as free as possible from such unpleasant feelings as tension, anger, and resentment. Therefore, they want to talk about these emotional things, resolve conflicts with their spouses, clear the air, and keep things pleasant between them.

Of course, no one is completely cognitive or completely emotional. We will all be somewhere on the spectrum this simple graph shows. If a person's personality and communication patterns tended to be almost completely emotional in manifestation, this person would appear on the left side of the graph. If a person exhibited a cognitive pattern of communication, he or she would be on the right side of the graphic. We all fit somewhere between the two extremes. Where do you fit in?

Emotional   **Cognitive**

Where would you say men and women tend to be on the chart? Right! As a general rule, women tend to be more emotional in their ways of dealing with other persons, especially spouses and children. Men tend to be more cognitive in their ways of communicating.

At this point, you may believe that being on the right side of the graph is more desirable than appearing on the left. This is a common misconception. The truth is that every type of personality has advantages and disadvantages. A person on the left side of the graph, who shares more feelings, is not necessarily less bright or less intellectual. This person is simply aware of his or her feelings and is usually better able to do something about them. On the other hand, a person on the right side of the graph, who does not display feelings, may simply be suppressing feelings and is therefore less aware of them.

A surprising fact is that the so-called cognitive person (on the right) is controlled by his feelings just as is the so-called emotional person, but *he doesn't realise it*. For example, the stiff, formal intellectual generally has deep feelings also, but uses enormous energy to keep them buried so he won't be bothered with them. But unfortunately they *do* bother him. Whenever someone (like an 'emotional' wife, or child) is around asking him for affection and warmth, he is not only unable to respond, but is angered that his precious equilibrium has been disturbed.

A father's initiative

'My husband, Fred, has been such a good provider and he's so respected,' Mary Davis explained to me in her bewilderment, 'that I feel terrible about how I feel toward him. I get so angry at him; then I feel so guilty I can't stand myself. I try to talk with him about how I feel about him and about the children. He becomes uncomfortable, clams up, then is mad at me. Then I'm upset and angry and get back at him – I even get frigid and can't make love with him. What can I do? I am so worried about my marriage and my children, but I can't even talk with my husband about it. How can our marriage last?'

There's the old story. Fred Davis is competent in the business world. He knows about his business. He has the facts. He is comfortable in a world where emotional factors are omitted and generally not needed. He is 'cognitive' in his communications. But at home he is like a fish out of water. He's married to a normal wife with normal womanly and wifely needs. Mary needs her husband's warmth and support. She needs him to share in her concerns, fears, and hopes. Mary tends to be 'emotional' in her communications. She needs to feel that her husband is willing to assume his responsibility for the family. These needs of hers are normal and do not mean that she is weak, overly sensitive, or that she is not carrying her own responsibilities. I have yet to see a truly happy, warm family where the husband and father did not assume family responsibilities. Again, the wife and mother has her responsibilities, but the husband must be willing to help her and support her in each of these. One reason that this is essential is that a woman has a difficult time initiating love for her husband when she feels her husband is not willing to support her 100 per cent in all areas of family life, emotional and otherwise. Of course, the same is true regarding the husband's family responsibilities. He must know that his wife is ready to help and even step in when needed.

Another way to put it is that when a woman must assume responsibilities because her husband simply won't, it is hard for her to feel secure and comfortable in his love. For example, one wife whom I was counselling complained that she felt insecure in her husband's love and had difficulty responding to him lovingly. As it turned out, she was responsible strictly by default for essentially every aspect of the family life, including the garden and handling the finances. This arrangement may be all right if husband and wife both agree and are happy with it; but even then, the husband must assume these overall responsibilities if needed; that is, he must be ready and willing to take over if the spouse is over-burdened. A husband's 'willingness' to be completely answerable for his family is one of the greatest assets a wife and child can have.

A wife can be wonderful at accepting love initiated by her husband, amplifying it manyfold, and reflecting it to him and the children, filling the home with an inexplicably wonderful climate. But a husband must take the responsibility of initiating love. Husbands who have found this secret are to be envied. The love returned to him by his wife is priceless, in my opinion the most precious commodity in this world. It is difficult to initiate love at first, but as the husband experiences his wife's love in return, he finds it to be multiplied many times, and sees that as this love increases with time, it becomes easier and easier to do.

If there are exceptions, I have yet to find one. The husband who will take full, total, overall responsibility for his family, and take the initiative in conveying his love to his wife and children, will experience unbelievable rewards: a loving, appreciative, helping wife who will be her loveliest for him; children who are safe, secure, content and able to grow to be their best. I personally have never seen marriage fail if these priorities are met. Every failing marriage I have seen has somehow missed these priorities. Fathers, the initiative must be ours.

But, you ask, how can a husband take initiative and responsibility for conveying love in the family when he is essentially cognitive and clumsy in the feelings area, and the wife is more competent in the emotional area? This is one of the most frequent, unrecognised, and difficult problems in marriage today. It is difficult to deal with, because most men, like Fred Davis, are not aware of the problems. Instead of seeing how vital the emotional life of his wife and children is, he sees it as an uncomfortable nuisance which should be avoided. The result, of course, is what we just experienced between Fred and Mary – frustration and bewilderment with a serious breakdown of communication.

It seems that everyone today realises how crucial communication is in family living. Can you see from Fred and Mary's relationship how communication bogs down when a 'cognitive' husband cannot talk on the emotional level, or an 'emotional' wife cannot share her innermost feelings and longings? What a dilemma! Husbands, we must face facts. The chances are overwhelming that our wives are more competent in the area of love, caring, and identifying emotional needs in us and our children. And we generally follow the guidance of experts, right? Then, clearly, we men desperately need our wives' help in leading us in this relatively foreign world of feeling.

Not only must a husband be willing to respect and be guided by his wife's natural know-how in emotional areas, he must encourage his wife and support her daily task of setting the emotional climate in the home. If he is a hindrance to her, insisting on handling matters without regard to her feelings, he will discourage her and eventually break her spirit. Oh, how many wives I have seen in counselling who have been thwarted by their husbands in efforts to feelingly love them and the children. These wives' spirits are broken, and the resulting depression is crippling.

But look at marriages where a husband appreciates his wife's deep feelings and her need to communicate them. He not only listens to her, he learns from her. He learns how rewarding and profoundly fulfilling and satisfying it is to share on the emotional level, whether it is pleasant or unpleasant. This is a marriage that grows over the years. A husband and wife become closer and invaluable to each other. Such a marriage is one of life's greatest gifts.

Is love blind?

'See? John doesn't love me anymore. All he does is criticise me,' complained pretty Yvonne. She and her husband were seeing me 'as a last resort' for marriage counselling. Yvonne continued, 'Isn't there anything good you can say about me, John?' Much to my surprise, John actually could think of nothing with which to compliment his wife. Yvonne was attractive, intelligent, articulate, and talented, but John seemed able only to point out discrepancies. They had been married six years. Why the apparent inconsistency?

It's hard to realise, when we think of the astounding divorce rate, that essentially all marriages begin with great hope, expectation, love, and wonderful feelings between the newlyweds. Initially all seems wonderful, the world is perfect. And the marriage of Yvonne and John began that way too. What a startling change! How could it possibly have happened?

One factor is *immaturity*. But what is immaturity? It does correlate somewhat with age, but not necessarily. Within the scope of this particular problem, immaturity can be defined as the inability to tolerate (or cope with) ambivalence on a conscious level. Ambivalence is simply having opposite or conflicting feelings toward the same person.

This explains the saying 'love is blind'. When we are first in love, and during the first weeks or months of our marriage, we must see our loved one as perfect, and we can tolerate no unpleasant feeling toward her or him. Therefore, we suppress (deny, ignore) anything we might not like in our spouse. We can then be aware of only his or her good points. Then we are oblivious to such things as an imperfect figure or physique, over-talkativeness, quietness, tendency to be fat or thin, over-exuberance, withdrawal, moodiness, lack of ability in sports, music, art, sewing, or cooking.

This hiding of our spouse's undesirable aspects from ourselves works beautifully at first. As we live with our loved one day in, day out, month in, month out, there are new discoveries about him or her. Some good and some not so good. Some even revolting. But as long as we keep suppressing the unpleasant into our unconscious, we can continue to see our dear one as a near-perfect model, and everything is fine.

One problem. We cannot keep on suppressing forever. Someday we reach a point of saturation. By that time we may have been married several days or several years. This depends on (1) our capacity to suppress, overlook, and ignore the unpleasant; and (2) our level of maturity, namely, our ability to deal consciously with our mixed feelings.

When we reach this critical point, we cannot continue to support the negative any longer. Suddenly we are faced with days/months/years of disagreeable feelings toward our spouse. Again, because of immaturity (inability to deal with ambivalence), we do a flip-flop. We suppress the good feelings and accentuate the bad. Now we see our spouse in an almost reversed aspect of being all bad with little or no good – overwhelmingly unpleasant or almost nothing pleasant.

And this can happen quickly. Two months ago John saw Yvonne as the epitome of perfection. Now he can barely tolerate her presence. Yvonne has remained essentially the same. John's perceptions of her have almost completely reversed.

How do we cope with this common problem that is plaguing our social structure and threatening the strength of our national fibre? As usual, the answer is easy to give, but difficult to carry out. First, we *must realise* that no one is perfect. It's amazing. We hear that statement every day, but we don't believe it. By playing the suppression game, we show that we want and expect perfection from our loved ones,

Second, we must keep ourselves continually aware of our spouse's assets and liabilities. I must realise and not forget that there are things about my wife for which I am grateful and things about her I wish were different – in this way she is like all other women. It's taken me a long time to learn to think of her delightful traits during times when I'm disappointed with her.

Third, we must learn to accept our spouses as they are, including their faults. The likelihood of finding someone or something better through divorce and another marriage, or in an affair, is remote, especially with the overwhelming guilt and other problems such action would produce. Remember that your wife or husband is truly irreplaceable.

Unconditional love

'Love is very patient and kind, never jealous or envious, never boastful or proud, never haughty or selfish or rude. Love does not demand its own way. It is not irritable or touchy. It does not hold grudges and will hardly even notice when others do it wrong. It is never glad about injustice, but rejoices whenever truth wins out. If you love someone, you will be loyal to him no matter what the cost. You will always believe in him, always expect the best of him, and always stand your ground in defending him' (1 Corinthians 13:4-7, TLB).

This clear statement tells us the foundation of all love relationships. The secret here can be called 'unconditional love' that is not dependent on such things as spouse performance, age, weight, mistakes, etc. This kind of love says, 'I love my wife, no matter what. No matter what she does, how she looks, or what she says, I will always love her.' Yes, unconditional love is an ideal and impossible to attain completely, but the closer I can come to it, the more my wife will be made perfect by God who loves us so. And the more He changes her to His likeness, the more pleasing she will be to me and the more I will be satisfied by her.

This brings us to the end of our discussion on marriage *per se*. We touched only a few points, but there are many fine books on the subject that one can obtain for further study. Now we want to move on to our primary task of learning how to love a child.

As we explore the world of a child, we must remember that the marital relationship remains unquestionably the most important bond in a family. Its effect on a child throughout his or her life is tremendous.

One example from my experience which bears this out involves a Christian family I saw in counselling. Pam, a fifteen-year-old girl, was brought to me by her parents because of sexual misconduct which resulted in pregnancy. The child was a beautiful girl with a delightful personality. She was talented in several areas. Pam had a strong, warm, healthy relationship with her father – a somewhat scarce commodity these days. Her relationship with her mother also seemed sound. At first I was baffled why Pam chose to become sexually involved in the way she did. She had little feeling or concern about the boy who fathered the child. And she was not of a temperament which would inappropriately seek male attention. Pam had always been a respectful, compliant child who was easy for her parents to manage. Then why did she suddenly become pregnant? I was stumped.

Then I saw the parents together and individually. You guessed it. Pam's parents had marital conflicts that were well hidden from others. These strifes were of a longstanding nature, but the family managed to function for years in a fairly stable way. And Pam had always enjoyed a close relationship with her father. As the child grew older, the mother became increasingly jealous of this bond. But other than this jealousy, the mother had a fairly supportive relationship with Pam.

Then Pam reached adolescence. As her physical features began changing into those of a woman, the mother's jealousy mushroomed. By various forms of nonverbal communication (which we will get into later), the mother relayed a message to Pam loud and clear. The message was that Pam was now a woman who could hereafter look after her own emotional needs, especially attention from the male population. As many girls of that age do, she attempted to substitute attention from male peers for her daddy's love. She was acting in accordance with her mother's subconscious, nonverbal instructions.

Pam's mother was aware of her own unhappy marital situation which resulted in a poor sexual life with her spouse. She was also aware of the closeness between Pam and her father. She was *not* aware of the intenseness of her jealousy toward Pam. And she was not aware of her role in Pam's sexual acting out.

In cases such as this, it is fruitless and many times harmful to confront each person (especially the mother in this case) with wrongdoing. Though the surface complaint was the child's behaviour, the basic problem was in the marital relationship. To help this family in the most supportive, loving, sensitive way, as their therapist, I had to help the parents in their marriage bond and not focus on faultfinding and judging their mistakes. I had to bring them to a point of receiving God's forgiveness in Jesus Christ. As the marital bond is mended in a case of this kind and guilt is resolved, this troubled mother-child relationship can be rectified.

This case illustration should show how important the marital union is in the life of a child. The stronger and healthier this bond is, the fewer problems we will encounter as parents. And the more effective will be the information in this book when it is applied.

Let's look now at the second most important relationship in the family.

3

The foundation

Real love is unconditional, and should be evident in all love relationships (see 1 Corinthians 13:4-7). The foundation of a solid relationship with a child is unconditional love. Only that type of love relationship can assure a child's growth to his full and total potential. Only this foundation of unconditional love can assure prevention of such problems as feelings of resentment, being unloved, guilt, fear, insecurity.

We can be confident that a child is correctly disciplined only if our primary relationship with him is one of unconditional love. Without a basis of unconditional love, it is not possible to understand a child, his behaviour, or to know how to deal with misbehaviour.

Unconditional love can be viewed as a guiding light in child rearing. Without it, we parents operate in the dark with no daily landmarks to tell us where we are and what we should do regarding our child. With it, we have indicators of where we are, where the child is, and what to do in all areas, including discipline. Only with this foundation do we have a cornerstone on which to build our expertise in guiding our child and filling his needs on a daily basis. Without a foundation of unconditional love, parenting becomes a confusing and frustrating burden.

What is unconditional love? Unconditional love is loving a child *no matter what*. No matter what the child looks like. No matter what his assets, liabilities, handicaps. No matter what we expect him to be and most difficult, no matter how he acts. This does not mean, of course, that we always like his behaviour. Unconditional love means we love the *child* even when at times we may detest his behaviour.

As we mentioned when discussing unconditional love in the marriage relationship, it is an ideal which we will never achieve 100 per cent of the time. But again, the closer we get to it, and the more we achieve it, the more satisfied and confident parents we will become. And the more satisfied, pleasant, and happy will be our child.

How I wish I could have said when our children were at home with us, 'I love my children all the time regardless of anything else, including their behaviour.' But like all parents, I could not. Yet I will give myself credit for having tried to arrive at that wonderful goal of loving them unconditionally. I did this by constantly reminding myself of the following:

1. They are children.
2. They will tend to act like children.
3. Much of childish behaviour is unpleasant.
4. If I do my part as a parent and love them despite their childish behaviour, they will be able to mature and give up childish ways.
5. If I love them only when they please me (conditional love), and convey my love for them only during those times, they will not feel genuinely loved. This in turn will make them insecure, damage their self-image, and actually prevent them from moving on to better

self-control and more mature behaviour. Therefore, their behaviour and its development is my responsibility as much as theirs.

6. If I love them unconditionally, they will feel good about themselves and be comfortable with themselves. They will then be able to control their anxiety and, in turn, their behaviour, as they grow into adulthood.

7. If I love them only when they meet my requirements or expectations, they will feel incompetent. They will believe it is fruitless to do their best because it is never enough. Insecurity, anxiety, and low self-esteem will plague them. They will be constant hindrances in their emotional and behavioural growth. Again, their total growth is as much my responsibility as theirs.

For my sake as a struggling parent in those years, and, for the sake of my sons and daughters, I prayed that my love for my children would be as unconditional as I could make it. The future of my children depends on this foundation.

A child and his feelings

Remember the simple graph in chapter 2? Where do you think we would find children on it? Right! Way over on the left side. A child comes into the world with an amazing ability to perceive emotionally. An infant is extremely sensitive to the feelings of his mother. What a beautiful thing to see a newborn infant brought to his mother for the first time, if the mother truly wants him. He conforms to the mother's body and the baby's contentment is obvious to all.

But a baby's first meeting with a mother who does not want him presents another picture. This infant is not content and frequently nurses poorly, frets a great deal, and is obviously unhappy. This also occurs when the mother is troubled or depressed, even though there is no discernable difference in the way the mother treats the infant.

So it is important to realise that from birth, children are extremely sensitive emotionally. Since their fund of knowledge is, of course, small, their way of communicating with their world is primarily on the feeling level. This is crucial. Do you see it? A baby's first impressions of the world are through his feelings. This is wonderful yet frightening when we think of the importance of it. An infant's emotional state determines how he sees or senses his world – his parents, his home, himself.

This sets the stage and foundation for almost anything else. For example, if a baby sees his world as rejecting, unloving, uncaring, hostile, then what I consider a growing child's greatest enemy – anxiety – will be harmful later to his speech, behaviour, ability to relate and to learn. The point is that a child is not only emotionally supersensitive but also vulnerable.

Almost every study I know indicates that every child wants to know of his parents, 'Do you love me?' A child asks this emotional question mostly in his behaviour, seldom verbally. The answer to this question is absolutely the most important thing in any child's life.

'Do you love me?' If we love a child unconditionally, he feels the answer to the question is yes. If we love him conditionally, he is unsure, and again, prone to anxiety. The answer we give a child to this all-important question, 'Do you love me?' pretty well determines his basic attitude toward life. It's crucial.

Since a child usually asks us this question with his behaviour, we usually give him our answer by what we do. By his behaviour, a child tells us what he *needs*, whether it's more love, more discipline, more accept-ance, or more understanding. (We'll get into this in detail later, but let's concentrate now on the irreplace-able foundation of unconditional love.)

By our behaviour, we meet these needs, but we can do this only If our relationship is founded on unconditional love. Note the phrase 'by our behaviour'. The feeling of love for a child in our heart may be strong. But it is not enough. By our behaviour a child sees our love for him. Our love for a child is conveyed by our behaviour toward that child, by what we *say* and what we *do*. But what we *do* carries more weight. A child is far more affected by our actions than by our words. More about this later.

Another critical concept for parents to understand is that each child has an *emotional tank*. This tank is figura-tive, of course, but in a sense very real. Each child has certain emotional needs, and whether these emotional needs are met (through love, understanding, discipline, etc.) determines many things. First of all, it determines how a child feels: whether he is content, angry, depressed, or joyful. Second, it affects his behaviour: whether he is obedient, disobedient, whiny, perky, play-ful, or withdrawn. Naturally, the fuller the emotional tank, the more positive the feelings and the better the behaviour.

Now here is one of the most important statements in this book: *Only if the emotional tank is full can a child be expected to be at his best or do his best.* And whose respon-sibility is it to keep that emotional tank full? You guessed it, the responsibility of the parents. A child's behaviour indicates the status of the tank. Later we'll talk about how to fill the tank, but now let's understand that this tank has got to be kept full, and only we parents can really accomplish it. Only if the tank is kept full, can a child really be happy, reach his potential, and respond appropriately to discipline. 'God, help me meet my child's needs as You do mine.' Philippians 4:19 says He will: 'And my God will meet all your needs.'

Children reflect love

Children may be conceptualised as mirrors. As the moon reflects the sun, children basically reflect love, but they do not initiate love. If love is given to them, they return it. If none is given, they have none to return. Unconditional love is reflected unconditionally, and conditional love is returned conditionally.

The love between Tom and his parents (chapter 1) is an example of a conditional relationship. As Tom was growing up, he yearned for a close, warm relationship with his parents. Unfortunately his parents felt that they should continually prompt him to do better by withholding praise, warmth, and affection except for truly outstanding behaviour, when he made them feel proud. Otherwise, they were strict, in that they felt too much approval and affection would spoil him and dampen his striving to be better. Their love was given when Tom excelled, but it was withheld otherwise. This probably worked well when he was very young; however, as he grew older, he began feeling that his parents didn't really love or appreciate him in his own right, but cared only about their own esteem.

By the time Tom became a teenager, his love for his parents strongly resembled that of his parents for him. He had learned well how to love conditionally. He only behaved in a way which pleased his parents when his parents did something to please him. Of course, with both Tom and his parents playing the game, eventually neither could convey love to the other because each was waiting for the other to do something pleasing. In this situation, each one becomes more and more disappointed, confused, and bewildered. Eventually depression, anger, and resentment set in, prompting the Smiths to seek help.

How would you handle that situation? Some would instruct the parents to demand their rights as parents: respect, obedience, and so on. Some would criticise Tom for his attitude toward his parents and demand that he honour them. Some would recommend severe punishment for Tom. Think about it.

Many children today do not feel genuinely loved by their parents. And yet, I've met few parents who do not love their children dearly. This is not just an academic question to think about and then say, 'That's too bad.' The situation is alarming. Dozens of religious cults or other devious organisations are a capturing the minds of thousands of our precious young people. How can these children so easily be brainwashed, turned against their parents and all other authority, and controlled by such bizarre doctrines? The main reason is that these young people have never felt truly loved and cared for by their parents. They feel that they were deprived of something, that their parents missed giving them something. What is it? Yes, unconditional love. When you consider how few children really feel properly cared for, loved, and comfortable, it is no wonder how far these cultish groups can go.

Why does this terrible situation exist? I do not believe parents per se should be blamed. When I talk with parents, I am gratified to find that most not only love their children, but are genuinely interested in what can be done to help *all* children. I find over and over again that the problem is that parents do not know how to *convey* their love to their children.

I am not pessimistic. As I lecture around the country, I am very heartened that today's parents not only listen, but are willing to expand themselves and their resources on behalf of their children. Many have changed their relationship with their children so that it is founded on scripturally based unconditional love. They have found that once this has been accomplished, their children's emotional tanks are filled for the first time. Parenting quickly becomes fulfilling, exciting, and rewarding. Then these fine parents have guidelines as to when and how to guide and discipline their dear ones.

How to convey love

Let's consider how to convey love to a child. As you remember, children are emotional beings who communicate emotionally. In addition, children use behaviour to translate their feelings to us, and the younger they are, the more they do this. It's easy to tell how a child is feeling and what frame of mind he's in simply by watching him. Likewise, children have an uncanny ability to recognise their parents' feelings by their behaviour, an ability most people lose as they reach adulthood.

On many occasions when my daughter was about sixteen she asked me such questions as, 'What are you mad at, Daddy?' when I was not even consciously aware that I was feeling a certain way. But when I thought about it, she was absolutely right.

Children are that way. They can so finely sense how you're feeling by the way you act. So if we want them to know how we feel *about them*, that we love them, *we must act like we love them*. 'Dear children, let us not love with words or tongue but with actions and in truth' (1 John 3:18).

As you realise, the purpose of the book is to examine how parents can put their feelings of love into action. Only in this way can they convey their love to their child so that he will feel loved, completely accepted, and respected, and able to love and respect himself. Only then will parents be able to help their children love others unconditionally, especially their future spouses and children.

Before we launch into discoveries of how to love a child, there must be one presupposition. It must be assumed that you are willing to apply what you learn. There is a difference between having a vague feeling of warmth toward a child, and your caring enough about him to sacrifice whatever is needed for his best interest. It is rather pointless to continue reading the book if you are not willing to seriously contemplate what it says, understand it, and apply its contents. Otherwise, it would be easy to read it superficially and conclude the information is simplistic and unrealistic.

Conveying love to a child can be broadly classified into four areas: eye contact, physical contact, focused attention, and discipline. Each area is just as crucial as the other. Many parents (and authorities) will focus on one or two areas and neglect the others. The area most overemphasised today, to the exclusion of the other three, is discipline. I see many children of Christian parents who are well-disciplined but feel unloved. In many of these cases the parents have unfortunately confused discipline with punishment, as though the two are synonymous. This is understandable, since I frequently read or hear authorities tell parents to use the rod and physically pinch a child with no mention of loving him. There is no mention of how to help a child feel good toward himself, his parents, or others, and no mention of how to make a child happy.

Every day I see the results of this approach to child-rearing. These children are well-behaved when they are quite young, although usually overly quiet, somewhat sullen, and withdrawn. They lack the spontaneity, curiosity, and childish exuberance of a love-nurtured child. And these children usually become behaviour problems as they approach and enter adolescence because they lack a strong emotional bond with their parents.

So we parents must focus on all areas of loving our children. Let's move on and discuss the first one – eye contact.

4

How to show love through eye contact

When you first think about eye contact, it may seem relatively unimportant in relating to your child. However, as we work with children, observe communications between parent and child, and study research findings, we realise how essential eye contact is. Eye contact is crucial not only in making good communicational contact with a child, but in filling his emotional needs.

Without realising it, we use eye contact as a primary means of conveying love, especially to children. A child uses eye contact with his parents (and others) to feed emotionally. The more a parent makes eye contact with his or her child as a means of expressing love, the more a child is nourished with love and the fuller is his emotional tank.

What is eye contact? Eye contact is looking directly into the eyes of another person. Eye contact is important in many situations. Have you ever tried to have a conversation with someone who keeps looking in another direction, unable to maintain eye contact with you? It's difficult. And our feelings toward that person are very much affected by this. We tend to like people who are able to maintain pleasant eye contact with us. Eye contact is pleasant, of course, when it is accompanied by pleasant words and pleasant facial expressions, such as smiling.

Unfortunately, parents, without realising it, can use eye contact to give other messages to a child. For instance, parents may give loving eye contact only under certain conditions, as when a child performs especially well and brings pride to his parents. This comes across to a child as conditional love, and as previously mentioned, a child cannot grow and develop well under these circumstances. Even though we may love a child deeply, we must give him appropriate eye contact. Otherwise, he will get the wrong message and not feel genuinely (unconditionally) loved.

It is easy for parents to develop the terrible habit of using eye contact primarily when they want to make a strong point to a child, especially a negative one. We find that a child is most attentive when we look him straight in the eye. We may do this mainly to give instructions or for reprimanding and criticising. This is a *disastrous* mistake, though using eye contact primarily in the negative sense works well when a child is quite young.

But remember that eye contact is one of the main sources of a child's emotional nurturing. When a parent uses this powerful means of control at his disposal in a primarily negative way, a child cannot but see his parent in a primarily negative way. And though this may seem to have good results when a child is young, this child is obedient and docile because of fear. As he grows older, the fear gives way to anger, resentment, and depression. Reread Tom's statements: this is what he is telling us.

Oh, if his parents had only known! They loved Tom deeply, but they were unaware that they seldom gave him eye contact, and when they did, it was when they wanted to give him explicit instructions or when disciplining him. Tom inherently knew that his parents somehow loved him. But, because of this way of using the critical ingredient of eye contact, Tom grew into his teen years confused and bewildered regarding his parents' true feelings toward him. Remember his statement, 'No one cares about me except my friends'? When I replied, 'No one?' he answered, 'My parents, I guess. I don't know.' Tom knew he should feel loved, but he did not.

An even worse habit parents may fall into is actually using the avoidance of eye contact as a punishment device. This is cruel, and we often do this to our spouses. (Come on, admit it.) Consciously refusing to make eye contact with a child is usually more painful than corporal punishment. It can be devastating. It can be one of those incidents in a child's life that he will never forget.

There are several types of circumstances between parent and child which can have lifelong effects, happenings that a child, and sometimes a parent, never forgets. The purposeful withdrawing of eye contact from a child as a way to show disapproval can be such a time and is obviously an example of conditional love. A wise parent will do all in his power to avoid it.

Our ways of showing love to a child should not be controlled by our being pleased or displeased. We must show our love consistently, unwaveringly, no matter what the situation. We can take care of misbehaviour in other ways – ways which will not interfere with our love-giving. We'll talk about discipline and how to do it without disrupting the love-bond. What we must understand at this point is that parents must use the eye contact as a continuous love-giving route, and not merely as a means of discipline.

We are patterns

We all know that children learn by role modelling: that is, patterning themselves after us. Children learn the art and use of eye contact this way also. If we give a child continuous, loving, positive eye contact, he will do the same. If we use eye contact as a way to display our annoyances, he will also.

Do you know a child who seems to be unpleasant or even obnoxious? Most likely he will look at you only briefly when he first sees you, and thereafter only when you have something particularly interesting to say or do. Other than that, he avoids looking at you. This fleeting eye contact is annoying, obnoxious, and aggravating. Now observe the way this child's parents use eye contact with him. Is there a similarity?

Imagine the distinct disadvantage this child has and will have throughout his life. Imagine how difficult it will be to develop friendships and other intimate relationships. How rejected and disliked he will be by his peers, not only now but probably indefinitely because the chances of his breaking this pattern of relating are bleak. First of all, he is not aware he's doing it; and second, changing this pattern is extraordinarily difficult, *unless the parents change their own pattern of eye contact before the child becomes too old.* This is a child's best hope.

A striking example of this tragedy was discovered in a research study on a pediatric ward in a general hospital. The researcher was sitting at one end of the corridor recording the number of times the nurses and volunteers entered each child's room. It was noted that some children were visited many times more often than others. The reasons were startling. It had something to do with the type of seriousness of the child's illness, of course, and with the amount of care required by the child. But this did not explain the great differences in the amount of contact with the patients. You've probably guessed it. The more popular children received more attention. Whenever nurses or volunteers had a free moment or a choice between which room to enter, they naturally picked children who could relate in the most pleasant way.

What made the difference in how pleasant these children were? There were several reasons, such as alertness, verbal ability, and spontaneity, but the most consistent factor was eye contact. The least popular children would initially look at the visitor briefly, then immediately look down or away. Subsequently, the children would avoid eye contact, making it difficult to relate to them. The adults would naturally be uncomfortable with these children. The nurses or volunteers, not realising their roles in initiating communication, would misunderstand them, assuming that the children wanted to be alone, or that the children did not like them. Consequently, they avoided these children, making them feel even more unloved, unwanted, and worthless.

This same thing happens in countless homes. It happened in Tom's. And it could have been corrected with regular, warm, pleasant eye contact (unconditional love) by the parents. If they had known this (and some other basic facts about loving children yet to be mentioned), they wouldn't have had these problems with Tom.

The Failure to Thrive Syndrome

Another important finding in our research studies also took place in a pediatric ward in a university hospital.

We were studying the strange phenomenon of the Failure to Thrive Syndrome. In this illness, a child, usually between six and twelve months of age, ceases to develop. Often he refuses food and stops growing, becomes listless and lethargic, and may actually die for no apparent reason. All tests and physical examinations are normal.

Why does a child lose his will to live? In most cases we know that the parents have rejected the child, often unconsciously (outside of their awareness). They are unable consciously to deal with their feelings of rejection toward their child, so unconsciously they reject him through their behaviour. In our study we found these parents avoided eye contact and physical contact with their child. Otherwise, they were good parents, providing such necessities as food and clothing.

The Failure to Thrive Syndrome is a startling phenomenon, but other findings are even more so. During the World War II Nazi blitzes of London, many young children were removed for their protection from the city and placed with adults in the countryside. Their parents remained in London. These children were basically well cared for physically, in that they were clean, well fed, and comfortable. Emotionally, however, they were severely deprived because there were not enough caretakers to give the emotional nurturing of eye contact and physical contact.

Most of these children became emotionally disturbed and handicapped. It would have been far better to have kept them with their mothers. The danger of emotional damage was greater than the danger of physical damage.

The danger and pitfalls awaiting an emotionally weak child are frightening. Parents! Make your children strong. Your greatest tool is *unconditional love.*

Eye contact and the learning process

In my work with the Headstart Programme, I enjoy teaching those wonderful teachers about eye contact and physical contact and how these affect anxiety and a child's ability to learn.

A teacher will identify a three-to-four-year-old child who is obviously anxious, fearful, and immature by the difficulty he has in making or maintaining eye contact. Mild to moderate emotional deprivation can cause a child to have difficulty with eye contact.

The extremely anxious child will, in addition, have problems approaching an adult (and often his peers). A normal emotionally nourished child will be able to approach the teacher by walking directly up to her, making full non-hesitating eye contact, and speaking what's on his mind – for instance, 'May I have a piece of paper?' The more emotionally deprived a child is, the more difficulty he will have in doing this.

In the average schoolroom it is not hard to find at least one child (usually a boy) who is so anxious and fearful that he cannot make good eye contact, speaks with great hesitancy (and frequently cannot speak without coaxing), and will come to his teacher with a side or oblique approach. Occasionally such a child will be able to approach his teacher only by walking almost backward. Of course these children have difficulty learning because they are so anxious and tense.

When we have found such an unfortunate child, I ask the teacher to teach him something while sitting across the table from him. Then I ask the teacher to hold the child, make occasional eye contact with him (as much as the child can tolerate) while talking with him. After a short while, I again ask the teacher to teach the child something while continuing to hold him. The teacher is amazed, and I am always amazed, at how much easier it is for the child to learn when his emotional needs are cared for first. With eye contact and physical contact, the teacher has eased the child's fears and anxiety, and increased his sense of security and confidence. This, in turn, enables him to learn better. Simple? Of course. Then why don't we do it more? For many reasons, I believe, ranging from a fear that we'll appear unprofessional, or fearing we'll spoil a child, to fearing we'll somehow damage him in some vague way. If there is anything we don't have to worry about, it's giving a child too much love.

In a new place

I am so thankful as a parent that I learned about the importance of eye contact. It has made a great difference with my own children. I'll never forget, for example, when we first moved to a new home. Our two boys were six and two at the time and were happy, energetic, and normally independent.

About a week after moving, we noticed a change coming over both boys. They were becoming whiny, clinging, easily upset, frequently fighting, constantly underfoot, and irritable. At that time, my wife Pat and I were furiously trying to get the house ready before I was to report to my new job. We were both becoming annoyed and irritated with the boys' behaviour, but figured it was because of the move.

One night I was thinking about my boys, and began to try to imagine myself in their place. The answer to their behavioural problems suddenly hit me like a hammer. Pat and I were with the boys night and day and talked to them frequently. But we were so intent on the housework that we never really gave them their rightful attention; we never made eye contact and seldom made physical contact. Their emotional tanks had run dry, and *by their behaviour* they were asking. 'Do you love me?' In their childlike, normally irrational way, they were asking, 'Do you love me now that we're in a new place? Are things still the same with us? Do you still love me?' This Is so typical of children during a time of change.

As soon as I understood the problem, I shared my thoughts with Pat. I think she was a bit incredulous at first, but by then she was ready to try anything.

The next day we gave the boys eye contact whenever we could, when they talked to us (active listening), and when we talked to them. Whenever possible, we held them and gave them concentrated attention. The change was dramatic. As their emotional tanks were filled, they became their happy, radiant, rambunctious selves and soon were spending less time underfoot and more time playing with each other and keeping themselves happy. Pat and I agreed that this was time well spent. We more than made up for it when the boys were out from underfoot, but more important, they were happy again.

It's never too early

Now one more illustration regarding the importance of eye contact. An infant's eyes begin focusing somewhere around two and four weeks of age. One of the first images which holds an infant's attention is a human face, but in particular he focuses on the eyes.

After a child is approximately six to eight weeks of age, you will notice that his eyes are always moving and seem to be searching for something. The eyes resemble two radar antennae constantly moving and searching.

Do you know what he's looking for? I think you already know: he's searching for another set of eyes. As early as two months, these eyes lock on another set of eyes. Already he is feeling emotionally, and even at this very early age his emotional tank needs to be filled.

Awesome, isn't it? It's no wonder that a child's way of relating to his world, and his feelings toward it, are so well formed early in his life. Most researchers state that a child's basic personality, modes of thinking, style of speech, and other critical traits are well fixed by the age of five.

We cannot start too early in giving a child continuous, warm, consistent affection. He simply *must* have this unconditional love to cope most effectively in today's world. And we have a simple but extremely powerful method by which to give it to him. It's up to each parent to use eye contact to convey unconditional love.

Though we have alluded to a child's need for physical contact, let's now explore the subject in some depth.

5

How to show love through physical contact

I t seems that the most obvious way of conveying our love to a child is by physical contact. Surprisingly, studies show that most parents touch their children only when necessity demands it, as when helping them dress, undress, or perhaps get into the car. Otherwise, few parents take advantage of this pleasant, effortless way of helping give their children that unconditional love they so desperately need. You seldom see a parent on his own volition or 'out of the blue' take an opportunity to touch his child.

I don't mean just hugging, kissing, and the like. I'm also talking about any type of physical contact. It is such a simple thing to touch a child on his shoulder, gently poke him in the ribs, or tousle his hair. When you closely observe parents with their children, many actually attempt to make the least possible physical contact. It's as if these poor parents have the notion their children are like mechanical walking dolls, the object being to get them walking and behaving correctly with the least assistance. These parents don't know the fantastic opportunities they are missing.

Within their hands they have a way of assuring their children's emotional security and their own success as parents.

It is heartening to see some parents who have discovered this secret of physical contact along with eye contact.

Scientists have discovered that touch plays a surprising role in our physical and mental well-being, and begins at birth, asserts an article 'The Sense That Shapes Our Future' in *Reader's Digest* for January 1992. The author, Lowell Ponte, points out that researchers at the University of Miami Medical School's Touch Research Institute showed that premature babies who received three fifteen-minute periods of slow, firm massage strokes each day showed forty-seven per cent greater weight gain than their ward-mates who did not get this attention. Premature babies who were massaged also exhibited improved sleep, alertness, and activity. Up to eight months later they displayed greater mental and physical skills.

Dr Michael Meaney, a psychologist at the Douglas Hospital Research Center at McGill University in Montreal, demonstrated that touching baby rats during the first few weeks of life results in development of receptors that control the production of glucocorticoids, powerful stress chemicals that cause a multitude of problems, including impaired growth and damage to brain cells. During his research, the article concluded, Dr Meaney's first child was born and in early childhood he made a point to hug her more than he otherwise would have done. 'Our evidence,' he was quoted as saying, 'suggests that the hugging I give my daughter today will help her . . . lead a happier, healthier life. My touch may be shaping her future.'

The article also pointed out that the caring touch of nurses and loved ones can do wonders for hospitalised patients, relieving anxiety and tension headaches and sometimes reduce rapid heartbeat and heart arrhythmias.

When our son David was eight, he played Peanut League Baseball. During the games I especially enjoyed watching one father who had discovered the secrets of eye and physical contact. Frequently, his son would run up to tell him something. It was obvious that there was a strong affectional bond between them. As they talked, their eye contact was direct with no hesitation. And their communication included much appropriate physical contact, especially when something funny was said. This father would frequently lay his hand on his son's arm, or put his arm around his son's shoulder and sometimes lovingly slap him on the knee. Occasionally, he would pat him on the back or pull the child toward him, especially when a humorous comment was made. You could tell that this father used physical contact whenever he possibly could, as long as he and the boy were comfortable and it was appropriate.

At times, this same father's teenage daughter would come to watch her brother play. She would sit with her father, either at his side or directly in front of him. Here again, this caring and knowledgeable father related to his daughter in an appropriate manner. He used much eye and physical contact but because of her age, did not hold her on his lap or kiss her (as he would have done if she were younger). He would frequently lightly touch her hand, arm, shoulder, or back. Now and then he would tap her on the knee or briefly put his arm around her shoulder and lightly jerk her toward him, especially when something funny happened.

Two precious gifts

Physical and eye contact are to be incorporated in all of our everyday dealings with our children. They should be natural, comfortable, and not showy or overdone. A child growing up in a home where parents use eye and physical contact will be comfortable with himself and other people. He will have an easy time communicating with others, and consequently be well liked and have good self-esteem. Appropriate and frequent eye and physical contact are two of the most precious gifts we can give our child. Eye and physical contact (along with focused attention, see chapter 6) are the most effective ways to fill a child's emotional tank and enable him to be his best.

Unfortunately, Tom's parents had not discovered the secret of physical and eye contact. They misused eye contact. They felt physical contact was all right for girls because 'they needed affection'. But Mr and Mrs Smith believed boys should be treated as men. They felt affection would feminise Tom into being a sissy. These grieving parents did not realise that the opposite is true, that the more Tom's emotional needs were met by physical and eye contact, especially by his father, the more he would identify with the male sex, and the more masculine he would be.

Mr and Mrs Smith also thought that as a boy gets older, his need for affection, especially physical affection, ceases. Actually a boy's need for physical contact never ceases, even though the type of physical contact he needs does change.

As an infant, he needs to be held, cuddled, fondled, hugged, and kissed – 'ooey-gooey love stuff' as one of my sons called it when he was in grade school. This type of physical affection is crucial from birth until the boy reaches seven or eight years of age – and I mean crucial! Research shows that girl infants less than twelve months old receive five times as much physical affection as boy infants. I am convinced that this is one reason younger boys (three years to adolescence) have many more problems than girls. Five to six times as many boys as girls are seen in psychiatric clinics around the country. This ratio changes dramatically during adolescence.

It is apparent then how important it is for a boy to receive just as much or more affection as a girl may need during the early years. As a boy grows and becomes older, his need for physical affection such as hugging and kissing lessens, but his need for physical contact does not. Instead of primarily 'ooey-gooey love stuff', he now wants 'boystyle' physical contact such as playful wrestling, jostling, backslapping, playful hitting or boxing, bearhugs, 'give-me-five' (slapping another person's palm in a moment of triumph). These ways of making physical contact with a boy are just as genuine a means of giving attention as hugging and kissing. Don't forget that a child *never* outgrows his need for *both* types.

As my boys, who are now grown, got older, they became less and less receptive to holding, hugging, and kissing. There were still times when they needed and wanted it, and I had to be alert in order to give it to them every chance I got. These times occurred usually when they had been hurt (either physically or emotionally), when they were very tired, when they were sick, and at special periods such as bedtime or when something sad had happened.

Remember the special moments discussed in chapter 4? Moments that are especially meaningful to a child, so meaningful that he will *never* forget them? These special opportunities to give our children affectionate physical contact (hugging, kissing), *especially as they get older*, are some of these very special times. These are the moments your child will recall when he or she is in the throes of deepest adolescence, when a teenager is in the conflict of rebellion on one hand versus affection for his parents on the other. The more special memories he has, the stronger he will be able to stand against adolescent turmoil.

These precious opportunities are limited in number. A child quickly passes from one stage to the next, and before we know it, opportunities to give him what he needs have come and gone. A sombre thought, isn't it?

Here is one other point about giving physical affection to boys. It is easier to give affection to a boy when he is younger, especially around twelve to eighteen months of age. As he grows older, however, it becomes more difficult. Why? One reason, as mentioned before, is the false assumption that the physical display of affection is feminine. The reason is that most boys become less appealing to people as they grow older. For example, to many people a seven- or eight-year-old boy is unappealing and irritating. In order to give a boy what he must have emotionally, we as parents must recognise these unpleasant feelings in ourselves, resist them, and go ahead with what we must do as mothers and fathers.

Let's now discuss the needs of girls in relation to physical contact. Girls generally do not display as much directness as boys to emotional deprivation during their first seven or eight years. In other words, they do not make their affectional needs so evident. I've seen many, many emotionally deprived children and, generally, it is very easy to tell which boys are suffering – their distress is usually obvious. But the girls seem better able to cope and are less affected by the lack of emotional nurturing *prior* to adolescence. Don't let this fool you. Although girls don't show their misery as much when they are younger, they suffer intensely when not properly cared for emotionally. It becomes quite evident as they grow older, especially during adolescence.

One reason for this lies in this matter of physical contact. Remember that physical contact, especially the more affectionate type (holding, hugging, kissing, etc.), is vital to boys during their younger years. The younger the boy, the more vital affectional contact is to him. While, with a girl, physical contact (especially the more affectionate type) *increases* in importance as she becomes older and reaches a zenith at around the age of eleven. Nothing stirs my heart more than an eleven-year-old girl who is not receiving adequate emotional nourishment. What a critical age!

Sharon's personality change

'I can't believe it! Sharon must be a Dr Jekyll and Mr Hyde,' exclaimed Mrs Francisco in her first visit with me concerning her fifteen-year-old daughter. 'She has always been a quiet, shy girl who never really acted up. In fact, she had to be prompted to do things, especially over the last few months. For a while I couldn't get her to do anything. She seemed bored with life. She lost interest in everything, especially her schoolwork. She seemed to lose all her energy. I took Sharon to her pediatrician, but he couldn't find anything wrong with her. Then I talked with the school counsellor and her teachers. They were also concerned with Sharon's attitude and boredom. Some friends told me not to worry, that it was a stage she'd grow out of. I hoped they were right but had my doubts. Then one day a friend of mine who has a daughter Sharon's age called. She said that her daughter thought Sharon was on drugs. I didn't think Sharon was the type, but I searched her room anyway and found some marijuana.

'For the first time in her life she acted horribly. She yelled and screamed at me, saying I was prowling and I had no right to intrude on her privacy. I was shocked at her defiance.

'That seemed to be the beginning of her personality change. Now she's angry all the time, just hateful. She demands to go out with the worst crowd in school, and it scares me to think of what they might be doing.

'Now all she cares about is being away from home with her gooney friends. What will become of her, Dr Campbell? We can't control her.'

'Is Sharon the same way with her father?' I asked.

'She's much better with him for some reason, but even he is finding it more and more difficult to reason with her. But he's not around much to help anyway. He's so busy. Gone most of the time. Even when he's here, he doesn't give us much time. The children adore him and want to be with him. But he immediately finds something they have done wrong and gets on to them about it. He really cares about the kids. I know he does. But that's his way.'

A tragic story. But a common one. A normal, well-endowed girl who for almost thirteen years was open, docile, easy to love. Like any child, her main concern was, 'Do you love me?' For almost thirteen years her parents had nearly continuous opportunity to answer her question and prove their love to her. As a typical girl, her need for demonstrable love increased over the years and hit a maximum around the age of eleven – that ultra critical age when girls have an almost desperate need for abundant eye contact, focused attention, and notably physical contact, especially from their fathers.

Preparation for adolescence

Why is affectionate love so important to girls around the age of pre-adolescence? The answer: preparation for adolescence. Every girl enters adolescence with some degree of preparation for it. Some are well prepared and some are poorly prepared.

The two most important aspects of this preparation for girls are self-image and sexual identity. At this point, let's look at sexual identity in a growing girl. You have read that a girl's need for affection increases as she grows older. As she nears adolescence she intuitively or unconsciously knows that how she weathers those turbulent adolescent years depends on how she feels about herself. It is vital for her to feel OK about herself as a female. If she is comfortable as a 'woman' when she enters adolescence (usually about thirteen to fifteen years old), her adolescence will be relatively smooth, pleasant, and comfortable with the usual ups and downs. The more stable and healthy her sexual identity, the better she will be able to withstand peer pressure. The less she thinks of herself as an 'OK female', the less stable she will be. She will then be more susceptible to pressure of peers (especially male peers) and less able to hold to parental values.

Sexual identity is self-approval as a female, and a girl gets her sexual identity at that age primarily from her father, as long as he is living and especially if he is in the home. If a father is dead or otherwise removed from relating to his daughter, a girl must find other paternal figures to fill these needs. But when a father has any viable relationship with her, he is the primary person who can help his daughter be prepared in this particular way for adolescence. What a great responsibility!

A father helps his daughter approve of herself by showing her that he himself approves of her. He does this by applying the principles we have discussed thus far – unconditional love, eye contact, and physical contact, as well as focused attention. A daughter's need for her father to do this begins as early as two years of age. This need, although important at younger ages, becomes greater as the girl grows older and approaches that almost magic age of thirteen.

One problem in our society is that as a girl grows older, a father usually feels increasingly uncomfortable about giving his daughter the affection she needs, especially when she becomes pre-adolescent (about ten or eleven years old). So as a daughter arrives at the age when she needs her father's affection the most, a father feels more awkward and uncomfortable, especially with physical contact. This is extremely unfortunate. Yes, fathers, we must ignore our discomfort and give our daughters what is vital to them for their entire lives.

Our Juvenile Court judge

Like most fathers, I had my difficulties giving my children everything they needed emotionally as they grew up – especially physical contact and focused attention for my teenage daughter Carey. Most evenings I came home from work physically and emotionally exhausted. After expending myself in my work, how could I find the energy and resources to give to my family, especially my daughter, at those times when they needed me? With my daughter, her need for me occurred when she had a bad encounter with her peer group, perhaps another girl being hostile toward her because of jealousy. Sometimes she didn't understand the cause of the jealousy and tried to find the fault in herself. On occasions such as this, I knew what I *should* do. I went to her room, talked with her about whatever was on her mind at the moment, gave her all the eye and physical contact she needed at the time, and patiently waited until she got around to sharing with me her pain and confusion. Then I could clarify her understanding of the whole situation. After a while the fact finally dawned on her that it wasn't anything she had done wrong or should blame herself for. Then she usually saw the situation clearly enough to avoid similar difficulties.

Anyway, that's the way I *liked* it to go, but I was seldom bursting with energy and enthusiasm to carry it out. Usually all I felt like doing was eating supper, sitting in my favourite chair, reading the newspaper, and relaxing.

Here is what helped me overcome this inertia. When my daughter (or one of my sons) needed me, and my whole body was drawn like a magnet to a chair or bed, I thought of a friend, a fine judge of the Juvenile Court. I deeply appreciated and respected the judge. One of the worst, most humiliating and tragic things that could possibly have happened to me or my family would have been to appear in his court with one of my children on, say, a drug charge. I said to myself, 'Campbell, one out of every six kids appears before the Juvenile Court. If you want to make sure one of your kids isn't included, you'd better hop to it and give them what they need instead of looking after yourself.' Just the thought of appearing before the judge with my child on some sort of charge was unbearable. It usually worked. I'd get off my backside and do what I knew I should do as a father.

Back to physical contact. One day in my parenting years, I was thinking how essential physical contact is and yet how most parents seem to consider it so basic and simplistic; we assume we are doing it when, in fact, we seldom do. I was groping for an illustration to point out this problem when my dear wife ran across an article about religious cults, including the Unification

Church (Moonies). A young man who was interviewed told of being brainwashed by the Moonies.

One of the most powerful techniques used was as follows. In an emotionally charged atmosphere and surrounded by several Moonies, the young man was required to think back into his childhood and remember painful moments. He told of an incident when he was three years old. He remembered feeling lonely and distressed, and tried to seek comfort in physical contact from his mother. His mother did not have time for him at that moment and he felt rejected. Then the Moonies embraced him (physical contact) repeatedly, stating that *they* loved him (implying of course that his mother did not).

Frightening, isn't it? The fact that there are dozens of such religious cults and other influences in our country today trying to capture the minds of our children is alarming enough. But even worse, they are able to do so because parents are failing to provide for basic emotional needs of their children by showing unconditional love.

Yet most parents do love their children. Again, the basic problem is that we are not aware that we must convey our love to our children *before anything else*: before teaching, before guidance, before example, before discipline. Unconditional love must be the primary relationship with a child, or everything else is unpredictable, especially their attitudes and behaviour.

But we should not be pessimistic about this. The really encouraging thing is that we know what the problem is and we know how to combat it. These are reasonable answers. I am convinced that most parents, because they love their child, can be *taught* to convey this love. The difficult question is, how can we get this across to all (or at least most) parents? This is something which all concerned parents must consider. The answer will require the input and action of many.

And in addition to learning to use eye contact and physical touch, parents must learn how to make use of *focused attention.*

6

How to show love through focused attention

E ye contact and physical contact seldom require real sacrifice by parents. However, focused attention does require time, and sometimes a lot of it. It may mean giving up something parents would rather do. Loving parents will detect when a child desperately needs focused attention and perhaps at a time when the parents feel least like giving it.

Just what is focused attention? Focused attention is giving a child full, undivided attention in such a way that he feels without doubt that he is completely loved. That he is valuable enough *in his own right* to warrant parents' undistracted watchfulness, appreciation, and uncompromising regard. In short, focused attention makes a child feel he is the most important person in the world in his parents' eyes.

Some may think this is going a bit too far, but take a look at Scripture and see how highly children are regarded. Notice the high priority Christ gave them: 'And they began bringing children to Him, so that He might touch them . . . and [He] said . . ., "Permit the children to come to Me . . ., for the kingdom of God belongs to such as these." . . . And

He took them in His arms and began blessing them, laying His hands upon them' (Mark 10:13-16, NASB).

Their value is also stressed in the Old Testament: 'Behold, children are a gift of the Lord' (Psalm 127:3, NASB) and (when Jacob answered Esau's question, 'Who are these with you?') 'The children whom God has graciously given your servant' (Genesis 33:5, NASB).

A child ought to be made to feel he is the only one of his kind. Few children feel this but oh, the difference it makes in that small one when he knows he is special. Only focused attention can give him that realisation and knowledge, it is so vital in a child's development of self-esteem. And it profoundly affects a child's ability to relate to and love others.

Focused attention, in my experience, is the most demanding need a child has, because we parents have extreme difficulty in recognising it, much less fulfilling it. There are many reasons we do not recognise this particular need. One of the main reasons is that other things we do for a child seem to suffice. For example, special favours (ice cream or sweets), gifts, and granting unusual requests seem to substitute for focused attention at the time. These kindnesses are good, but it is a serious mistake to use them as a stand-in for genuine focused attention. I found it a real temptation to use this type of substitution because favours or gifts were easier to give and took much less of my time. But I found over and over again that my children did not do their best, did not feel their best, and did not behave their best unless I gave them that precious commodity, focused attention.

The tyranny of the urgent

Why is it so difficult to give focused attention? Because it takes *time*. Numerous studies have been done and books written showing that time is our most precious possession. Put it this way. Even if you could give twenty-four hours a day, seven days a week, it is virtually impossible to fulfil all of your obligations. That is a true statement. It is not possible for you to take care of every obligation and every responsibility in your life as you would like it to be done. You *must* face up to that fact. If you do not, you will naively assume that everything will somehow get taken care of, and when you assume that, you will become controlled by the tyranny of the urgent. Urgent matters will then automatically take precedence in your life and control your time. Unfortunately, they usually are not. Take the sacred telephone, for example. I say sacred because it takes precedence over almost all else. The ringing telephone must be answered regardless of time, place, or situation. Your family may be having a few wonderful moments together at supper time. In our home when our children were with us, this was of the highest importance to me. But if the telephone rang, it was given almost a sacred right to interfere with, disrupt, and even destroy our family fellowship. It shows how the tyranny of the urgent wins out over the important things of life once again.

You know, there is just not enough time in our short lives to be controlled by the urgent and be able to look after the important. We can't have our cake and eat it too. So what can we do about it? I'm afraid there is only one answer. And it isn't simple or easy. We must determine our priorities, set our goals, and plan our time to accomplish them. *We* must control our time in order to take care of the important things.

Set priorities

What are the priorities in your life? Where does your child fit in? Does he take first priority? Second? Third?

Fourth? You must determine this! Otherwise, your child will take a low precedence and suffer from some degree of neglect.

No one else can do this for you. A spouse cannot determine your child's priority in *your* life. Nor can your minister, counsellor, employer, or friend. Only you can do this. So what is it, fellow parent? What and who gets priority in your life? – Job? Church? Spouse? House? Hobby? Children? Television? Social life? Career?

In almost all families that have found contentment, satisfaction, happiness, and genuine thankfulness among all family members, the parents possess a similar priority system. Usually their first priority is of an ethical nature, such as a strong religious faith or moral code. In most cases, this is manifested by placing God first in their lives and having a warm, comforting, loving, supportive relationship with Him. They use this stabilising relationship to influence all other relationships. Their second priority is the spouse, as discussed previously. The children take priority number three. As you can see, real happiness is found in family orientation – spiritual family then physical family. God, spouse, children. These are essential. The remaining priorities are important, of course, but these three must come first.

I have talked with many people who sought contentment in such things as money, power, and prestige. But as they experienced life and discovered real values, they sadly realised they were investing in the wrong account. I've seen numerous wealthy persons who spent their better years making it. Tragically, they had to seek counselling when they realised that, despite their wealth and power, their lives were pathetically and painfully empty. Each would weep and consider his or her life a 'failure' because of a wayward child or a spouse lost through divorce. He or she realised only then that the only worthwhile possession in life is someone who loves you and cares what happens to you – God, spouse, and child.

People who are terminally ill, I have noticed, come to the same conclusion. As they look back on life, they too know that the only thing that really matters is whether someone genuinely cares for and unconditionally loves them. If these individuals do have such loved ones, they are content. If they do not, they are to be pitied.

I once talked with the wife of a minister, a most beautiful woman who had incurable cancer. She was such a radiant wholesome person. As we talked, she explained how, since she had known of her illness, her outlook on life had been transformed. With the knowledge of impending death, her priority system was forced to change. For the first time she realised there was not enough time in the life of *any* parent to provide for the needs of spouse and children if less important things were not resisted. The minister's wife gave her husband and children first priority, and what a difference was evident in their lives. Of course, this does not mean we should neglect other areas of our lives, but we must control the time we spend on them and their influence on us.

Fleeting moments

This illustration poignantly points out the importance of focused attention. I read of a father who was sitting in his living room one day. It was his fiftieth birthday, and he happened to be in an irritable mood. Suddenly his eleven-year-old boy Rick bounced into the room, sat on his father's lap and began kissing him repeatedly on the cheeks. The boy continued his kissing until his father sharply asked, 'What are you doing?' The child answered, 'I'm giving you fifty kisses on your fiftieth birthday.' Ordinarily the father would have been touched by this loving act of affection. Unfortunately, because he was depressed and irritable, he pushed the boy away and stated, 'Let's do that some other time.' The boy was crushed. He ran out of the house, jumped on his bike, and rode away. A few moments later the child was struck and killed by a car. You can imagine the grief, remorse, and guilt suffered by this poor father.

These stories tell us several things. First, because life is so unpredictable and uncertain, we cannot know or plan how many opportunities we will have for nurturing our children, especially times to give focused attention. We must take advantage of our timely opportunities because they are fewer than we may realise. Our children are growing up.

Second, these moments of opportunity do not happen every day. Remember those special moments which leave a lasting impression on a child? That moment when Rick tried to kiss his father fifty times was one such priceless moment. If the father had been able to spend those few moments with Rick in a positive way. Rick would have affectionately remembered that time the rest of his life, especially when tempted to act against parental values, as, for example, in the dissident days of adolescence. However, if Rick had not been killed, he would never have forgotten the pain, anguish, and humiliation of that moment.

Let's look at another story regarding focused attention. In the diary of the father of a great humanitarian was found a description of a day spent fishing with his son. The father laments how the day was a 'total loss' because the son seemed 'bored and preoccupied, saying very little.' The father even wrote that he probably would not take his son fishing again.

Many years later a historian found these notes, and with curiosity compared them with the entries of the same day in the son's diary. The son exclaimed what a 'perfect day' it had been, 'all alone' with his father. He described how deeply meaningful and important it was to him.

The goal of focused attention

What is it that defines focused attention? When a child feels, 'I'm all alone with my mummy (or daddy)'; 'I have her (him) all to myself; 'at this moment, I'm the most important person in the world to my mother (father)'; this is the goal of focused attention, to enable a child to feel this way.

Focused attention is not something that is nice to give our child only if time permits; it is a critical *need* each child has. How a child views himself and how he is accepted by his world is determined by the way in which this need is met. Without focused attention, a child experiences increased anxiety because he feels everything else is more important than he is. He is consequently less secure and is impaired in his emotional and psychological growth. Such a child can be identified in the nursery or classroom. He is less mature than children whose parents have taken the time to fill their need for focused attention. This unfortunate child is generally more withdrawn and has difficulty with peers. He is less able to cope and usually reacts poorly to any conflict. He is overly dependent upon the teacher or other adults with whom he comes into contact.

Some children, especially girls deprived of focused attention from their father, *seem* to be just the opposite. They are quite talkative, manipulative, dramatic, often childishly seductive, and are usually considered preco-cious, outgoing, and mature by their kindergarten and infant school teachers. However, as these girls grow older, this behaviour pattern does not change and becomes gradually inappropriate. By the time they are eight or nine they are usually obnoxious to their peers and teachers. However, even at this late date, focused attention, especially from the fathers, can go a long way in reducing the children's self-defeating behaviour, decreasing their anxiety, and freeing them to resume their maturational growth.

How to give focused attention

Now that we've seen how vital focused attention is to a child, how do we accomplish it? I have found the best way to give a child focused attention is to set aside time to spend with him *alone*. If you're already thinking how difficult it is to do this, you are right. Finding time to be alone with a child, free from other distractions, is what I consider to be the most difficult aspect of good child rearing. You might say this separates the best parents from other parents; the sacrificing parents from the non-sacrificing; the most caring from the least caring; the parents who set priorities from those who do not. Let's face it, good child rearing takes *time*. Finding time in our hyperactive society is hard, especially when children often are addicted to television and sometimes would rather spend time with it. This is all the more reason focused attention is so crucial. Children are being influ-enced by forces outside the family more than anytime in history. It takes tremendous effort to pry time from busy schedules, but the rewards are great. It is a wonderful thing to see your child happy, secure, well liked by peers and adults, and learning and behaving at his best. But believe me, fellow parent, this does not come automatically. We must pay a price for it! We must find time to spend alone with each child.

John Alexander, former president of InterVarsity Christian Fellowship, related at a conference some years ago how difficult it was for him to find time for each of his four children. His solution was to save at least one half-hour every Sunday afternoon for each of his children. Everyone must find his own way of doing this.

My time during our parenting years was also difficult to manage. I tried to conserve it as much as possible for my children. For example, when my daughter was taking music lessons close to my office Monday afternoons, I scheduled my appointments so that I could pick her up. Then we would stop at a restaurant for supper. At these times, without the pressure of interruption and time schedules, I was able to give her my full attention and listen to whatever she wanted to talk about. Only in this context of being alone without pressure can parents and their child develop that special indelible relationship which each child so desperately needs to face the realities of life. It's such moments as these that a child remembers when life becomes difficult, especially during those tumultuous years of adolescent conflict and the normal drives for independence.

It's also during times of focused attention that parents can take special opportunities to make eye contact and physical contact with a child. It is during times of focused attention that eye and physical contact have stronger meaning and impact upon a child's life.

Of course, it is more difficult to find time for focused attention when there are several children in the family. I remember counselling a seven-year-old girl for numerous problems she was having at school and at home –

problems with school work, peer relationships, sibling relationships, and immature behaviour. You've perhaps guessed that her parents had not given her focused attention. She had nine brothers and sisters and her parents couldn't give her the focused attention she needed. Actually, they weren't aware that this girl was suffering from lack of focused attention because all of their other children were quite well adjusted. The parents were farmers, and during the natural course of a day – milking, feeding the animals, and ploughing – they spent sufficient time alone with each child to forestall problems. With this particular child, because of her age, individual chores, and birth order, the natural course of events prevented her from enjoying enough of her parents' attention. She felt neglected and unloved. Her parents loved her dearly, but the child did not feel it and so she did not know it.

Careful planning pays off

This illustration indicates how important it is to *plan* our time in order to provide focused attention for *each* child. This is difficult. In a two-child family, each parent is often able to spend time with one of the children. With more than two children, the problem becomes progressively more difficult. And, of course, in a one-parent family the logistics are more difficult. However, careful planning pays off. For example, on a particular day (say next Friday) one child may be invited to a party, another may be at a relative's, leaving one child free. A careful parent whose children take priority would consider this time a golden opportunity to give focused attention to that child. Of course, our plans must consider the emotional needs of each and every child, or we'll have the same problem as in the ten-child farm family just mentioned.

This is especially difficult when we have both a demand-ing and a nondemanding child in the same family. We must resist the concept that the loudest squeaking hinge gets the oil. Every child has the same needs whether he demands they be met or not. Especially vulnerable in this regard is a nondemanding, passive child who also is a middle child. And if his siblings happen to be demand-ing children, his parents will find it all too easy to pass him by until problems develop.

Watching for unexpected opportunities yields addi-tional time. For example, times occur when a parent finds himself alone with a child, a time perhaps when the others are outside playing. Here is another opportu-nity to fill that child's emotional tank and prevent prob-lems brought on by a dry one. This time of focused attention may be quite short: just a moment or two can do wonders. Every moment counts. It's like making deposits in a savings account. As long as the balance is healthy, a child's emotional life will be sound and he will have fewer problems. It's also an investment in the future, especially the years of adolescence.

Every deposit is assurance that a child's teenage years will be healthy, wholesome, pleasant, and rewarding for both child and parent. The stakes are high. What's worse than a wayward adolescent son or daughter? What's more wonderful than a well-balanced teenager?

Of course, long periods of focused attention are important also. As children grow older, this time of focus needs to be lengthened. Other children need time to warm up, let their developing defenses down, and feel free to share their innermost thoughts, especially anything that may be troubling them. As you can see, if these times of focused attention were begun early in a child's life, he accepts it very naturally and finds it much easier to share emotional things with his parents. On the other hand, if times for focused attention are not provided, how can a child learn to communicate meaningfully with his parents? Again, the stakes are high. What is worse than having a troubled child who can't share his feelings with you? What is more wonderful than for your child to be able to bring anything to you to talk over?

All this is difficult and takes time. But many people I've met have shared with me all sorts of ways they have done this. I remember listening to the late Joe Bayly, a Christian writer and publishing executive, talk about this. He marked off definite times on his appointment calendar to spend with his family, and when someone called and asked him to accept a speaking engagement at that time, he politely told the inquirer that he had another engagement.

Joe Bayly had another good way to give his children focused attention. He had personal flags for each family member. Each flag was designed to suit the personality of the child for whom it was designated and was given to the child on his or her birthday. Thereafter it was flown on the flagpole in front of the house on special occasions, for example, subsequent birthdays, when that child would return home after trips, or going away to university. This is an example of indirect focused attention.

When others are present

We mentioned that focused attention is given when alone with a child, away from other family members. Although this is true, there are times when focused attention must be given with others present. This is especially true when a child is ill, has experienced some emotional pain, or for some other painful reason has regressed. By regressed, I mean he is in poor control of his feelings and/or behaviour.

Here is an example of this. One day, deeply concerned parents sought my advice regarding their twelve-year-old son Tim. The boy's first cousin, also a twelve-year-old boy had come to live with them. The cousin was a very demanding child who had overshadowed Tim by taking almost all his parents' attention. Tim felt displaced by his overpowering cousin, became depressed, withdrawn, and occasionally uncommunicative. Part of my advice to the parents was, of course, to give both Tim and his cousin much focused attention; that is to spend time with Tim alone and the cousin alone. However, the cousin continued to clearly dominate each situation when the two boys were present. Next, I advised the parents to give each boy focused attention whenever the cousin was being overly dominant. The parents were able to do this by turning directly toward Tim when it was his turn to speak, giving him full eye contact, and physical contact when convenient, and responding to his comments. Then when it was appropriately Tim's cousin's turn to speak, the parents repeated the process with him.

This type of focused attention usually works well only if a child is also receiving ample focused attention alone. By the way, I've taught teachers these simple principles which have revolutionised their teaching and perceptions toward each child.

Focused attention is time consuming, difficult to do consistently, and many times burdensome to already exhausted parents. But focused attention is the most powerful means of keeping a child's emotional tank full of investing in his future.

7

Appropriate and inappropriate love

Let's consider the *too-much-love* controversy. Some contend that too much love will spoil a child, while others claim you can't love a child too much. The confusion in this area often causes advocates of both sides to take an extreme position. Many of the former group are severe disciplinarians, and many of the latter group are over indulgent.

Consider the issue in light of the concept of *appropriate love*, which will provide healthy nurturing and foster a child's emotional growth and self-reliance. The picture then quickly becomes dearer. We can then hold to the principle that a child needs a superabundance of appropriate love but no inappropriate love.

Inappropriate love

We may define *inappropriate love* as affection which, when conveyed to a child, hinders a child's emotional growth by failing to meet a child's emotional needs, and which fosters an increasingly dependent relationship upon a parent and hampers self-reliance.

The four most common types of inappropriate love are possessiveness, seductiveness, vicariousness, and role-reversal. Let's take them one at a time.

Possessiveness

Possessiveness is a tendency of parents to encourage a child to be too dependent on his parents. Paul Toumier, noted Swiss counsellor, deals with the subject quite well in his article, "The Meaning of Possessiveness'. He states that when a child is small, dependency is 'obvious and almost complete.' But if this dependency does not diminish as a child grows older, it becomes an obstacle to a child's emotional development. Many parents try to keep their children in a state of dependence upon them. Dr Toumier states that they do this 'by suggestion or by emotional blackmail,' or else by using their authority and insisting upon obedience. The child is theirs. They have rights over him because he belongs to them. Such parents are termed *possessive*. These parents tend to treat their child as an object or property to be possessed or owned, and not as a person who needs to grow in his own right and to become gradually independent and self-reliant.

A child must have respect from his parents to be himself. This does not, of course, mean no limit-setting or being permissive. (Every child needs guidance and discipline.) It means to encourage a child to think to be spontaneous, to realise he is a separate person who must assume more and more responsibility for himself.

If we parents disregard a child's right to gradually become independent, one of two things will happen. He may become overly dependent on us and overly submissive, failing to learn how to live in his world. He may become easy prey to strong-willed, authoritative personalities or cultish groups; or there will be deterioration of our relationship with a child as he gets older. He will become more resistant to our guidance.

Again, as Dr Toumier suggests, we should 'possess as if not possessing.' Such is the great message of the Bible. Man can never truly possess anything. He is but the steward of the goods that God entrusts to him, for 'the earth is the Lord's, and everything in it' (1 Corinthians 10:26, NIV).

Of course, there is some possessiveness in every parent. But we must take care to (1) identify it within ourselves; (2) separate it from true concern for a child's total welfare, especially concerning his need to become self-reliant; (3) be as continually aware of it as we can; and (4) resist its influence.

Seductiveness

The second inappropriate way of expressing love is through seductiveness. I have to start out by saying this is a difficult subject to write about because *seductiveness* is not easy to define. The word seems to be used to communicate everything from elicitation of sexual experience to pollution.

Regarding our subject at hand, I believe it sufficient to define seductiveness as attempting consciously or unconsciously to derive sensual/sexual feelings from an encounter with a child.

An example of this was discussed at a recent seminar on child psychiatry. A seven-year-old girl was seen at a psychiatric clinic for frequent masturbation and poor school performance. The evaluation disclosed that the child spent much time fantasising (day-dreaming) her mother's death and living alone with her father. It was also noted that her father spent much time holding the child, caressing and fondling her in such a way that seemed to bring sensual enjoyment to both father and child. When these facts were gently shared with the father, his response was, 'Oh, my word, I just realised that when I wash the soap off of her when we're showering together, she reacts like a mature woman.' This was a case where the father was obviously seductive. However, he apparently did not fully realise what he was doing. As in almost all cases of this sort, the marital relationship in this family was hurting. In families where the marriage is not healthy, it is not uncommon for seductiveness to exist. In our day the problem is worsening.

What do you think of this letter to Ann Landers which appeared in her syndicated column some years ago?

> Dear Ann Landers: I don't know if I have a problem or not. It's our beautiful twelve-year-old daughter. I've seen girls who are crazy about their fathers, but never anything quite like this.
>
> Donna sits next to (or on top of) her father at every opportunity. They play with each other's hands and act kittenish like a couple of goofy kids. She hangs on her father when they walk or their arms are around one another's waists. Is this normal?
>
> Signed, Me Worried.

Are you a parent of a preadolescent daughter? What do you think? Does this sound good or bad? Would you be worried? What would you do?

Here is Ann Lander's reply:

> Dear W: Sounds to me as if there's entirely too much touching. Today a girl of twelve is more of a woman than

a child. Donna needs to be talked to, but it would be better if the word did not come from you.

Perhaps an enlightened relative or an adult friend could tell Donna it is unbecoming and unhealthy for a young girl to have so much physical contact with her father. (Surely this behaviour has been observed by others.)

If you know of no person you might call on to communicate the message tactfully but firmly, by all means enlist the help of the school counsellor. I believe Donna should be approached rather than your husband. He is apt to be resentful and defensive.

I would like to reply to Ann's reply. I agree that it does sound like there is too much physical contact here, and it does sound seductive. However, this is the mother's viewpoint, and the chances are overwhelming that the marital relationship is poor. In short, neither we (nor Ann) know for sure if there is actually sensual seduction here or not. Perhaps this situation is similar to the one at the end of chapter 2 where the mother is jealous of a good relationship between daughter and father.

Supposing the relationship here is indeed a seductive one, would you go to a twelve-year-old girl and suggest that her own father was sexually improper with her? Genuine respect for parents is hard enough to find today without further undermining it.

But nonetheless there is one principal comment I'd like to make regarding Ann's reply and that is that it exemplifies the general mentality today regarding loving children. Her advice seems to suggest that, because the father was conveying his love to the child inappropriately, he should not show it at all. We have already seen how vital physical contact is to a preadolescent girl. This particular father was not doing it correctly. Is the answer to stop the physical contact completely?

I'm afraid this type of reaction has become generally accepted by our society. It is assumed that because some parents are seductive with their children, physical contact should be held to a minimum or actually be avoided. An analogy would be this: because I saw an obese person today, I should not eat at all, or at least minimally.

Another reason many parents unfortunately avoid physical contact with their children is that they may actually feel some sexual response to them. This can happen to any parents, especially fathers of older daughters. So this is indeed a dilemma. On the one hand, the child desperately needs to feel loved and physical contact is essential for this. On the other hand, the parents feel uncomfortable and fear this would be wrong or perhaps damaging to the child.

I think many loving parents would be greatly helped in this difficult area if they realised that: (1) every child regardless of age needs *appropriate* physical contact; (2) to have some occasional sexual feelings or fleeting sexual fantasies regarding a child is normal; (3) a parent should ignore these inappropriate feelings, go ahead, and give a child what he (or she) needs, including appropriate (non-seductive) physical contact.

With this confusion is it any wonder so few children feel genuinely, unconditionally loved?

Another fear many parents have regarding seductiveness is homosexuality. There seems to be a misconception that too much love expressed from mother to daughter or from father to son will lead to homosexuality, but just the opposite is the case.

It's not infrequent during my work in schools for a teacher to approach me with this concern. A woman teacher recently asked, 'Dr Campbell, I love my daughter so very much that I kiss her a lot and sometimes on the lips. Am I making a lesbian out of her?' After asking for other information to make sure the relationship was healthy, my answer was, 'Keep it up.'

Two examples

Let me give you two other examples. The second example will show what appropriate love, including physical contact, does for a child concerning sexual identity. But the first example concerns what the *absence* of it causes.

The first example is drawn from Rusty, a dear friend of mine who is mean, tough, 'all man', and a drill instructor in the US Marine Corps. He and his wonderfully warm sensitive wife have four boys, 'stair steps'. Rusty decided his boys were going to be like him, tough and rugged men. He treated them like Marine recruits with strict and rigid discipline – no affection, unquestioned obedience, and no questions.

Your reaction to this is important. How do you think his four sons developed? Do you think they are following in their father's footsteps? Do you think they're becoming 'all men'?

The last time I saw these boys each one was extremely effeminate. Their mannerisms, speech, and appearance were those of girls. Surprised? You shouldn't be. I see it every day. Boys with rejecting, harsh, nonaffectionate fathers generally become effeminate.

Here's the second example. Several years ago we had a pastor who was a huge man with rugged features. His very presence demanded attention, and he had a warm, loving heart. His boy at that time was three years old, the same age as my David but a head taller and about

twenty pounds heavier, a 'spittin' image of his ol' man.'
Our pastor loved his son deeply and warmly. He was
very affectionate with the boy, lots of holding, hugging,
kissing, and wrestling.

How do you think this boy developed? Did he follow
in his father's footsteps? You bet he did. That little fellow
was just like his father. He had a strong, healthy sexual
identification and was secure, happy, lovable, and all
boy. He will do all right in this world with a dad like that.

If these two examples don't convince you that a
superabundance of appropriate love is not only war-
ranted, but needed by every child (girls *and* boys) from
each parent, let me give you this one fact. In all my reading and experience, I have never known of one sexually
disoriented person who had a warm, loving, and affectionate father.

So, due to these misconceptions we've just looked at
(and others), few parents are able to properly nourish
their children emotionally. Although there is abundant
love in their hearts, there is little in practice. I am convinced that once these misconceptions are corrected, and
once parents understand what a child needs, most are
able to provide the superabundance of appropriate love
each child must have.

Vicariousness

The third most common type of inappropriate love is
vicariousness. *Vicariousness*, or vicarious love, is living
one's life or dreams through the life of a child. One of the
most harmful kinds of Vicariousness is a mother's living
out romantic fantasies or longing through her daughter.
A mother does this by steering her daughter into relationships and situations where she herself longs to be. A

clue to this phenomenon is a mother's obsessive interests in the intimate details of her child's dating experiences, becoming sensually excited as her daughter reveals them to her. The destructiveness of this process is obvious. A child can be led into situations which she does not have the maturity or experience to handle. Pregnancy is just one possible consequence. Another frequent outgrowth of this is a degrading reputation for the child. Such a reputation can injure a child's self-image and self-respect for life.

This type of vicariousness can also happen between father and son with similar consequences. A father who acts out his own sexual prowess through his son's conquests is harming not only his son but others involved in his life. In this way the boy is heavily influenced to view women primarily as sexual objects. He will find it difficult to relate to women as persons with feelings, and especially as equals.

Of course there are many varieties of vicariousness. The kind just described happens to be the most destructive.

Another example of vicariousness is a father using his son to satisfy athletic longings of his own. To see this phenomenon in action, go to your nearest junior football game. A vicariously oriented parent becomes emotionally involved in the game to such an extent it is as though he himself were the player. You can see him becoming outrageously angry at the referee when the decision is against his son. Worst of all such a parent will reprimand and demean his son when he makes a mistake.

What does this bring to mind? The old problem of conditional love. The more vicarious we are with our children, the more our love for them is conditional upon how well they have performed and have met our own vicarious needs.

But lets face it. We're all vicarious to some extent, aren't we? When our David played junior league football, I considered him a pretty good player. As I sat there watching him, for some strange reason my mind drifted back to my professional football days. I would find myself recalling how desperately I wanted to make it to the major leagues. The pain and disappointment of failing to accomplish this focused before me as I watched David play so well. I wonder why. What a mistake it would have been if I vicariously attempted to fulfil my lost dream through my son.

Vicariousness becomes harmful when it modifies our love so that it is given in relation to a child's behaviour and is, in fact, conditional love. We parents must not let our own hopes, longings, and dreams determine the type of love a child receives.

Vicariousness can be considered a kind of possessiveness if it causes us to view children as possessions to be used to fulfil our own dream. How can a child grow in his own right and think for himself and rely on himself in this situation?

We must keep our love for a child unconditional. We must love him so that he can fulfil God's plan for his life, not our vicarious ones.

Role-reversal

Role-reversal was described some years ago by M.A. Morris and R.W. Gould in their Child Welfare League publications. They define this 'as a reversal of the dependency role, in which parents turn to their infants and small children for nurturing and protection.'

Brandt Steele and Carl Pollock present a description of role-reversal in the book. *The Battered Child* (Chicago:

University of Chicago Press, 1974, p 95). They state: 'These parents expect and demand a great deal from their infants and children. Not only is the demand for performance great, but it is premature, dearly beyond the ability of the infant to comprehend what is wanted and to respond appropriately. [These] parents deal with the child as if he were much older than he really is. Observation of this interaction leads to a clear impression that the parent feels insecure and unsure of being loved, and looks to the child as a source of reassurance, comfort, and loving response. It is hardly an exaggeration to say the parent acts like a frightened, unloved child, looking to his own child as if he were an adult capable of providing comfort and love . . . We see two basic elements involved – a high expectation and demand by the parent for the child's performance and a corresponding parental disregard of the infant's own needs, limited abilities, and helplessness – a significant misperception of the infant by the parent.'

Role-reversal is the primary relationship in the frightening phenomenon of child abuse. An abusing parent feels his child must take care of the parent's emotional needs, that the parent has a right to be comforted and nourished by his child. When the child fails in this, the parent feels a right to severely punish him.

Child abuse is the extreme form of role-reversal, but all parents use role-reversal to some extent. Sometimes when we ourselves are not feeling well, either physically or mentally, we expect our child to make us feel better. We may be depressed, physically ill, mentally or physically exhausted. At these times we have little or no emotional nurturing to provide our child. It can then be very difficult to give him eye contact, physical contact, or focused attention. When our emotional or physical resources are drained, we need nurturing ourselves. In this condition its so easy to make the mistake of expecting our child to be comforting, reassuring, compliant, mature in his behaviour, and passively obedient. These are not the characteristics of a normal child. If made to assume this unnatural role, a child will not develop normally. The list of possible disturbances which can result is endless.

We parents must not allow such a situation to develop. We must understand that parents do the nurturing, and a child receives it. During times when we are unable to carry this out, we must not look to our children to parent us. Of course, they can help us as they are able, running errands and getting things for us when we're sick, but they must not be expected to nurture us emotionally.

We should make every attempt to prevent times when we are unable to nurture our children. This may mean better care of our bodies to prevent illness and fatigue, for example – a sensible diet, plenty of rest, and plenty of exercise. It may mean looking out for our emotional health by engaging in hobbies or other refreshing activities to prevent depression or mental exhaustion. It may mean keeping our spiritual life fresh and exciting by allowing ample time for prayer and meditation. Most importantly, it means keeping our marriages strong, healthy, and secure. God should be first and one's spouse second and our children a close third. Remember, we will be able to give more to our child if we keep ourselves emotionally and spiritually replenished. This gets back to setting priorities and planning toward goals.

Don't toss the baby out with the bath water

We have looked at the four most common types of inappropriate love and several common misconceptions. Of course, these are ways of relating which we want to avoid. They are good neither for the child nor the parent.

However, as we avoid these mistakes, let's not 'toss out the baby with the bath water.' Let's not make a worse mistake and withhold *appropriate* love from our child. This is the most common of all child rearing mistakes. Far more children suffer from the lack of appropriate love than from exposure to inappropriate love.

Appropriate love is for the benefit and welfare of the child. Inappropriate love serves the abnormal needs and hang-ups of the parent.

We must face it. Our children have essential needs which only parents can fill. If we find we cannot fill these needs, if we cannot keep their emotional tanks full, if we can't give them an abundance of eye contact, physical contact, and focused-attention appropriately, we had better get help, and fast. The longer we wait, the worse the situation will become.

8

A child's anger

A nger is a natural response with all of us, including young children. Yet handling anger in a child is, in my opinion, perhaps the most difficult part of parenting. And because it is difficult, most parents respond to a child's anger in wrong and destructive ways.

Consider this. When a child becomes angry, he is quite limited in ways to express his anger. He has only two choices – to express the anger in behaviour or verbally. Both ways make it difficult for a parent to know how to respond properly.

If a young child expresses his anger, for instance, by banging his head, throwing toys, hitting, or kicking, such behaviour should be dealt with. On the other hand, if a child expresses anger verbally, it will almost certainly come across to the parent as unpleasant, disrespectful, and inappropriate. And this way of showing anger likewise is intolerable and unacceptable. What can a parent do?

Like steam in a kettle, anger must come out some way. No one, including a young child, can suppress anger and continue to keep it all inside. This is one of the most destructive things we can force a young child to do. If we refuse to allow a child to express anger in any way, he then must push the anger deeper and deeper within, causing destructive problems later in life. If the child is punished for expressing his anger either verbally or behaviourally, he has no other choice but to suppress the anger and bottle it up inside. As a result, this child will never be able to learn to handle anger maturely.

I call this the 'punishment trap'. As parents, we need to understand that punishment in itself is not the way to teach our children how to handle their anger.

Another easy mistake parents make in the face of childhood anger is to explode and dump a load of anger on an angry child. Children are helpless in the face of parental anger. They have no defence against it. A common example is found in such a harsh rebuke as, 'I never want to see you acting that way (or talking that way to me) again! Understand!' When a parent yells and screams at a child, he or she effectively closes off all normal ways for the child to express anger, and, as previously pointed out, the child must keep the anger inside and add the parent's anger to it.

Doubtless, the vast majority of parents today are not doing a good job in handling anger in their young children. If a child's anger comes out behaviourally or verbally, he is either punished or angrily scolded, or both. Again, since these are the only ways a child can express anger, the treatment forces suppressed anger.

Why is this so destructive? Because, as pointed out, the anger eventually must come out some way. If suppressed too much, the anger will come out as 'passive-aggressive behaviour'. Passive-aggressive (PA) behaviour is basically unconscious (out of the child's awareness) and anti-authority. It is an unconscious motivation on the part of the child to upset authority figures (parents and teachers, especially) by doing the opposite of what is expected of them. Once passive-aggressive features start influencing a child's behaviour, discipline becomes a nightmare.

Passive-aggressive behaviour, the opposite of an open, honest, direct, and verbal expression of anger, is an expression of anger that gets back at a person indirectly. A few simple examples of this are procrastination, dawdling, stubbornness, intentional inefficiency, and forgetfulness. The subconscious purpose of PA behaviour is to upset the parent or authority figure and cause anger.

Passive aggressive ways of handling anger are indirect, cunning, self-defeating, and destructive. Unfortunately, since passive-aggressive behaviour is subconsciously motivated, a child is not consciously aware that he is using this resistant, obstructive behaviour to release pent-up anger to upset his parents.

One of the ways a small child can early show PA tendencies is by soiling his pants after he has been toilet-trained – a very effective but unhealthy way to express anger. In most cases, the parents have prohibited expression of any anger, especially verbally. There is little parents can do in such a situation. The parents have backed themselves into a corner. The more the parents punish the child, the more he will soil his pants, to subconsciously upset the parents. What a dilemma, God pity both parent and child in such a situation.

Many school-aged children use PA to express anger by making poorer grades than those of which they are capable. Their attitude is much like 'You can lead a horse to water, but you can't make him drink.' For a PA child who uses poor grades to make his parents angry, its 'You can make me go to school, but you can't make me get good grades.' Again, with PA behaviour the parents are helpless; the child's anger is in control and not visibly showing. The more the parents become upset – the subconscious purpose of all this – the worse the situation becomes.

It is important to again emphasise that a PA child does not do things consciously or purposefully to anger authority figures. They are part of an unconscious process of which he is not aware, and into which he has been forced by the 'punishment trap'.

Passive-aggressive behaviour is very common. Why? Because most people do not understand anger or know what to do with it. They feel that anger is somehow wrong or sinful and should be 'disciplined' out of a child. This is a serious misunderstanding, because the feeling of anger is normal; every human being through the ages has felt anger, including Jesus, who became angry with those who misused the temple. If when your child becomes angry and you spank him or yell at him, 'Stop that kind of talk! I will not allow it,' or as some scream, 'Shut up or I'll smack you!' What can the child do? Only two things – he can disobey and continue to 'talk that way', or obey you and 'stop talking that way'. If he chooses the latter and ceases to express his anger, the anger will simply be suppressed; and it will remain unresolved in his subconscious, waiting to be expressed later through inappropriate and/or passive-aggressive behaviour.

Another mistake some parents make related to the suppression of anger is the inappropriate use of humour. Whenever a situation becomes tense, especially if someone is becoming angry, some parents will tease and try to interject humour to relieve the tension. Of course, humour is a wonderful asset in any family. But where it is consistently used to escape the appropriate handling of anger, children simply cannot learn to appropriately deal with it.

Passive-aggressive behaviour easily becomes an ingrained, habitual pattern which can last a lifetime. If a child into his mid-teen years avoids honestly and openly dealing with anger in an appropriate manner, he may use passive-aggressive techniques in relationships throughout life. This can affect his relationships later with spouse, children, work, associates, and friends. PA behaviour is also the primary force behind drugs, inappropriate sex, school failure, running away, and suicide. What a tragedy! And most of these unfortunate people are hardly aware of their self-defeating pattern of behaviour or their problems with handling anger.

Passive-aggressive behaviour is the worst way to handle anger for several reasons: (1) it can easily become an ingrained tenacious pattern of behaviour which will last a lifetime; (2) it can distort a person's personality and make him/her a quite disagreeable person; (3) it can interfere in all the person's relationships; (4) it is one of the most difficult behavioural disorders to treat and correct.

Scripture instructs parents to train a child in the way he should go. Forcing a child to suppress the anger and not deal with it properly is training him in the way he should not go. It is crucial to train a child in the proper way to handle anger. This is done by teaching him to resolve the anger, not suppress it.

Teaching our children and teenagers to handle anger is what I truly consider to be the most difficult part of parenting. First, it is most difficult because it does not come naturally. As we have discussed, our natural response to a child's anger is becoming more angry than the child and dumping the anger back on the child. Second, teaching the proper way to handle anger is difficult because it is a long, tedious process. As a goal, we want our child to handle his anger maturely by the age of sixteen or seventeen. It is a slow process because the handling of anger is a *maturational* process. An immature adult handles anger immaturely; a mature adult handles anger maturely. Passive-aggressive behaviour is the most immature way of handling anger. The most mature ways of handling anger are *verbally, pleasantly*, and resolving the anger toward the person at whom we are angry if at all possible.

No child can be expected to learn to handle this anger quickly. A wise parent realises that the well-parented child will very gradually learn these critical lessons as he goes from one developmental stage to another. Not until the child becomes six or seven or even older can he be expected to learn specifically how to handle anger maturely. Until that time, we as parents must avoid passive-aggressive behaviour taking root in our child. When the child is able, we can then specifically train our child to handle this anger more and more maturely as he gets older. This subject is far too extensive to cover adequately in this brief chapter. However, it is thoroughly covered in the book *Kids Who Follow, Kids Who Don't*.

Ephesians 6:4 says, 'Fathers, do not provoke your children to anger, but bring them up in the fear and admonition of the Lord.' Study this and also carefully read the following chapters in this book on discipline. Be careful to use punishment as a last resort and refrain from dumping your anger on your child. Parents, please do all in your power to remain pleasant with your child and yet be appropriately firm. If there are two words that sum up Christlike parenting, they are: *pleasant* and *firm*.

Pleasant includes loving kindness, optimism, and refraining from instilling fear or anxiety in the child, especially with our own anger. *Firm* includes fair expectations with consistency. Firmness does not mean rigidity and inflexibility. It considers the child's age, abilities, and maturity level.

Then when your child reaches adolescence, read *How to Really Love Your Teenager*, chapters 6 and 7, which will give you further guidance for that age. This includes how to train your child to handle anger maturely at least by the time he is sixteen or seventeen. Any PA behaviour beyond that age can be permanent.

Yes, teaching a child to handle anger is difficult, but one of the most important responsibilities in parenting today. As parents, we must be serious about this and be quite careful that we truly know what we are doing. Too much is at stake!

9

Discipline: what is it?

P eriodically, when I lecture on parent-child relationships for churches and civic groups, we spend three
or four hours talking about how to love a child before we
deal with discipline. Invariably, after two or three hours,
a parent will come up to me and say, 'I've enjoyed the lecture series so far, but when do we get to discipline? That's
where I have problems and need answers.'

This poor parent has usually misunderstood (1) the
relationship between love and discipline and (2) the
meaning of discipline. He has separated love from discipline in his mind as though they are two separate entities.
No wonder this parent is confused and has problems
controlling his child.

Parents who are confused in this way have usually
assumed that discipline means punishment (chastise-
ment according to some).

Both of these assumptions are false. I stress to those
parents and I hope to stress to you, fellow parent, that
love and discipline cannot be separated, and that punishment is a very small part of discipline.

The first fact parents must understand in order to
have a well-disciplined child is that *making a child feel*

loved is the first and most important part of good discipline.
Of course, this is not all but it is most important.

What you have read thus far in this book is the most
important aspect of discipline, and must be applied to
expect the best results from disciplining your child. There
is no point in reading further at this time if you have not
applied what you have already read, and if you have not
kept your child's emotional tank full. If you have not
made an effort to make your child feel loved with an
abundance of eye contact, physical contact, and focused
attention in an appropriate way, *please do not read further
but go back and reread the previous chapters.* The results will
disappoint you. Application of behavioural control techniques without a foundation of unconditional love is
barbaric and unscriptural. You may have a child who is
well-behaved when he is young, but the results are most
discouraging in the long run. Only a healthy love-bond
relationship lasts through all of life's crises.

What is discipline?

Now just what is discipline? What is your definition? In
the realm of child rearing, discipline is *training* a child in
mind and character to enable him to become a self-
controlled, constructive member of society. What does
this involve? Discipline involves training through every
type of communication. Guidance by example, modelling, verbal instruction, written requests, teaching, providing learning and fun experiences. The list is quite
long.

Yes, punishment is on this list, but it is only one of
many ways of discipline and is the most negative and
primitive factor. Unfortunately, we must use it at times
and we will discuss its use further. At present, it should

be re-emphasised that guidance toward right thought and action is far superior to punishment for wrong action.

With a clear definition of discipline in mind, consider it again in relation to unconditional love. *Discipline is immeasurably easier when the child feels genuinely loved.* This is because he wants to identify with his parents, and is able to do so only if he knows he is truly loved and accepted. He is then able to accept his parents' guidance without hostility and obstructiveness.

If a child does not feel genuinely loved and accepted, however, he has real difficulty identifying with his parents and their values. Without a strong, healthy love-bond with his parents, a child reacts to parental guidance with anger, hostility, and resentment. He views each parental request (or command) as an imposition and learns to resist it. In severe cases, a child learns to consider each parental request with such resentment that his total orientation to parental (and eventually to all) authority is one of doing exactly the opposite of what is expected of him. This type of emotional disorder is increasing at an alarming rate in our country, and children from Christian families are not excluded.

You are by now likely realising how crucial unconditional love is for good discipline (training). The more you keep your child's emotional tank full, the more he will respond to discipline (training). The less full his emotional tank, the less he will respond to discipline (training).

One aspect of appropriate love not yet mentioned is focused (active) listening. Focused listening is listening to a child in such a way that he is sure you know what he is trying to communicate to you. When your child knows you understand how he feels and what he wants, he is much more willing to respond positively to discipline, especially when you disagree with him. Nothing frustrates a child more than to be told to do something when he feels his parents don't understand his position. This does not mean catering to your child's demand or whim; it simply means listening to your child so that he doesn't feel you have ignored his thoughts and feelings, when you use your authority. Is that unreasonable? If you believe it is, you are not regarding your child as a valuable, separate person.

Think about it. When your child feels you have considered his position and feelings, you have assuaged your anger and resentment which would come back to haunt you later. Doesn't your Heavenly Father do as much for you? Christ said, 'Ask, and you will be given what you ask for. Seek, and you will find. Knock, and the door will be opened. For everyone who asks, receives. Anyone who seeks, finds. If only you will knock, the door will open. If a child asks his father for a loaf of bread, will he be given a stone instead? If he asks for fish, will he be given a poisonous snake? Of course not! And if you hardhearted, sinful men know how to give good gifts to your children, won't your Father in heaven even more certainly give good gifts to those who ask Him for them?' (Matthew 7:7-11, TLB).

To give a child focused listening requires at least eye contact, with physical contact and focused attention if possible and if appropriate. Acknowledging that you understand your child (even if you disagree with him) is usually helpful. Repeating your child's thoughts and feelings back to him is a good way to ensure that he understands that you understand. Your child's thoughts and feelings may make a difference in your own understanding and actions also.

I recall an incident with our then 16-year-old Carey. Pat and I gave her permission to go to a wrestling match at her high school on a school night with three of her friends. She was told to come home right after the match. The match was to end around 10 o'clock. It usually takes thirty to forty-five minutes to make the trip. At 11 o'clock I became concerned; at 11:15 I called the parents of one of the boys. They said the group had stopped by there to get a car with snow tyres (bad weather had begun) and the parents offered them a snack. The kids had left home about 11:10. Carey arrived home at 11:40.

I was angry. I sent her to bed after giving her a lecture about responsibility, and placed her on one week's restriction (she was grounded). Why did I react without listening to what Carey had to say? I was thinking more of myself than the actual situation. I wasn't feeling well that night and wanted to get to bed early. I had a busy schedule the next day. Secondly, my daughter was later than I expected, and she did not call to tell us that she would be late. I assumed she was totally negligent in the whole situation.

I have a wise daughter. She waited until the next day when I had recovered my composure and loving ways before giving me all the facts. She also knew that I listen better when I am not angry. As it turned out the kids took a longer but safer way home. Ice and snow were making the roads slippery. She was telling the truth; it all checked. Where she had been negligent was failing to call us when she saw that she would be later than we expected. After apologising to her for over-reacting, I decreased the restriction to be commensurate with what she had done.

There are two lessons we can learn from this experience. The first is the importance of really listening to a child when he or she is communicating. I could have saved myself frustration and my daughter's pain and possible anger and resentment toward me by listening to her before acting.

The other lesson is the importance of controlling our emotions at such times. I do believe that a mother or father's worst enemy in raising a child is uncontrolled feelings, especially anger. As in my experience, this can cause a parent to say or do things he or she will regret later. Too much anger, especially uncontrolled anger, will frighten a child initially. It may even seem to help a child's behaviour, but this is only temporary. As a child grows older, parental expression of too much anger (temper outbursts) will instil increased disrespect for the parents along with kindling a child's own anger and gradual resentment. When you stop to think about it, uncontrolled feelings draw disrespect from anyone. Why should we expect otherwise from our spouse or child?

You know as well as I that we all lose our cool at times. One thing to remember is that when we do, we shouldn't be afraid to apologise later after things have calmed down. It's very possible to make something beautiful out of something bad. It's amazing how pleasant communication can become when a family member is big enough to apologise when he is wrong, and losing one's calm inappropriately (over-reacting) can be such an occasion. Believe it or not, the times of warmness and closeness that usually follow this are among those special moments that a child (and parents) never forgets. They are priceless.

Emotional overreactions, however, can only be tolerated in a family to a limited extent, especially if no apology takes place. They should be kept to a minimum. How is this accomplished?

Control your anger

It's important to remember that anger is difficult to control under certain conditions. Some of these are (1) when a person is depressed; (2) when a person is afraid; (3) when a person is physically not well; (4) when a person is fatigued mentally or physically; and (5) when a person's spiritual life is not healthy.

A book could be written on coping with each of these problems. For now it must suffice to warn each parent to look out for himself mentally, emotionally, physically, and spiritually. Unhealthiness in any of these areas can hamper the parent-child relationship, the marital relationship, in fact, all relationships, primarily by hurting our ability to control our anger. Lets get in shape. Uncontrolled anger is detrimental to good discipline.

Discipline and punishment

I hope you are realising that you may have much to do before you can expect your child to respond well to discipline. Anyone can beat a child with a rod as the primary way of controlling his behaviour. That takes no sensitivity, no judgement, no understanding, and no talent. To depend on corporal punishment as the principal method of discipline is to make that critical error in assuming that discipline equals punishment. Discipline is *training* the child in the way he should go. Punishment is only one part of this, and the less the better. Please remember this statement: *the better disciplined a child is, the less punishment will be required.* How well a child responds to discipline depends primarily on how much the child feels loved and accepted. So our biggest task is to make him feel loved and accepted.

There are several reasons why so many parents fall into the punishment trap, why they somehow get the idea that their greatest responsibility in discipline (training a child) is to spank (punish) him.

One reason parents fall into this trap is because so many books, articles, seminars, institutes, radio programmes, sermons, and papers advocate corporal punishment while glossing over or bypassing all other needs of a child, especially love. Few plead for a child and his real needs. Too many today are dogmatically calling for children to be punished, calling it discipline, and recommending the harshest, most extreme form of human treatment. Most perplexing of all, many of these advocates call this a biblical approach. They quote three verses from the Book of Proverbs (13:24; 23:13; 29:15) to totally justify beating a child. They neglect to mention the hundreds of Scripture verses dealing with love, compassion, sensitivity, understanding, forgiveness, nurturing, guidance, kindness, affection, and giving, as though a child has little or no right to these expressions of love.

Proponents of corporal punishment seem to have forgotten that the shepherd's rod referred to in Scripture was used almost exclusively for *guiding* the sheep, not beating them. The shepherds would *gently* steer the sheep, especially the lambs, by simply holding the rod to block them from going in the wrong direction and then gently nudge them toward the right direction. If the rod was (or is) an instrument used principally for beating, I would have a difficult time with Psalm 23, 'Thy rod and Thy staff, they comfort me' (v 4, KJV).

I have not noticed one of these advocates state that there might be times when punishment may be harmful. So many parents have come away from these gatherings or readings with the idea that corporal punishment is the primary, or even the only way to relate to a child.

The results of this approach

I have seen the results of this approach. Children who were passive, compliant, very quiet, withdrawn, and easily controlled when they were young, lacked a strong, healthy, love-attachment to their parents, and gradually became defiant, resentful, difficult to control, self-centred, nongiving, nonaffectionate, insensitive, nonforgiving, noncompassionate, resistant to authority, and unkind as adolescents.

I think Scripture is quite helpful here. The Apostle Paul instructed, 'And, fathers, do not provoke your children to anger; but bring them up in the discipline and instruction of the Lord' (Ephesians 6:4, NASB). What has happened to these dear children just described? Yes, they were provoked to anger by mechanical, harsh discipline (primarily punitive) without the foundation of unconditional love. I like *The Living Bible* paraphrase of the Ephesians passage: 'And now a word to you parents. Don't keep on scolding and nagging your children, making them angry and resentful. Rather, bring them up with the loving discipline the Lord Himself approves, with suggestion and godly advice.'

Have you noticed that one deceptive trait of a young child who is disciplined primarily with punishment? Yes, he is easily controlled. That is the other reason so many parents fall into the trap. When a child is young, his behaviour can usually be well controlled by corporal punishment alone. That is, if you consider good behaviour as submissive compliance, lack of spontaneity, lack of self-confidence, and anxious docility.

You may be surprised, but I have seen many young children who were raised with much punishment especially corporal punishment, but who were unmanageable. These unfortunate children would be spanked severely, but the spankings would have no effect, and the children often would not even cry. Of course before coming to me, many parents have tried every piece of advice given to them, from trying to give even more punishment (like pinching the trapezius muscle), to not giving sweets, to putting the children in certain types of rigidly structured nursery schools. In every case, one of the problems was a lack in the parent-child love bond. These children just didn't feel genuinely loved and accepted. At that early age, resentment and defiance can develop to such an extent from a lack of unconditional love that not even corporal punishment can subdue these responses.

Put the horse before the cart

First things first, fellow parents. Practice uncontrolled love, *then* discipline. Putting the horse before the cart will create a positive relationship between parents and child and will keep *negative* interactions such as corporal punishment to a minimum. Notice that I did not say unconditional love will abolish the need for corporal punishment. How I wish it could, but it won't. The more genuine and unconditional the love-bond from parents to child, the more positive is the relationship, minimising the need for punishment. Unfortunately, punishment is required at times, and we'll explore that together later.

To summarise, in order for a child to respond well to discipline (training), we parents must give him what he needs. A child can learn (train) well only if he is happy, feels safe, content, confident, secure, accepted, and loved. Expecting a child to learn, namely, be disciplined, without our giving him what he needs is cruel enough.

But then to beat him for not living up to our expectations? We treat our pets better than that.

Consider this: An aggressive junior high school football coach once threatened to beat my then thirteen-year-old Carey with a paddle for what he considered an infraction in the school cafeteria. I called a school official and asked him if his school system actually allowed children to be beaten (especially teenage girls by male teachers with all the sexual connotations connected with such an act). He answered yes. When I asked him if he beat his dog he said he didn't. We wonder why children are becoming more and more disrespectful and resistant to authority. Can you figure it out?

The corporal punishment trap

One important reason why using corporal punishment as a principal means of behavioural control is dangerous is that it drastically alleviates guilt. Corporal punishment degrades, dehumanises, and humiliates a child. As a result, a child may feel the beating is punishment enough in itself. If the corporal punishment is instituted with enough frequency and severity, there will not be sufficient guilt provocation to enable a child to develop an adequate conscience. Without the foundation of unconditional love, the required developmental phases, especially proper parental identification, will fail to evolve, further crippling the development of a healthy conscience.

Many forget the important positive factor of guilt and consider it to be an unwanted feeling. Too much guilt is harmful, but a proper amount is vital in the formation and maintenance of a normal conscience. A normal, healthy conscience which keeps a child's behaviour within normal boundaries is far better than control by fear, and preferable to poor control or no control at all. What do you think enables a happy, well-adjusted teenager to control his behaviour? Right – his conscience. If you want your child to develop a normal responsive conscience which will enable him to *control himself*, then refrain from building your relationship with him on a punitive basis – by controlling his behaviour primarily by spanking and scolding, especially spanking.

Another tragic consequence of corporal punishment is called *identification with the aggressor*. It is also a guilt-escaping mechanism. A child identifies (sides with) the punishing parent, coming to the place where he feels being aggressive and punitive is right. Then, of course, this child grows up, has children, and treats them as he himself was treated. This is why abusing parents were themselves usually ill-treated by their parents. This use of corporal punishment (or the threat of it) as the main way of handling a child is passed on from generation to generation. This in itself is bad enough. With the frightening advent of violence in all modes of mass communication, especially television, is it any wonder that child abuse and all other forms of violence have become a national disgrace? Until we parents begin to proclaim the indispensable needs of a child, namely, unconditional love and loving discipline, the situation will continue to become worse. We must stand against the avalanche of demanding critics who insist that beating a child (confusing punishment with discipline) should be the primary way of relating to him. Are you aware that some of the critics do not have children themselves? Until we give a child what he desperately needs, he (and we) will suffer.

Dear parents, look at every statistic regarding children and adolescents in our nation today – academics, attitudes, respect for authority, emotional disturbance, motivation, drugs, crime, and so on. The situation is horrible. I maintain that the principle reason for our national dilemma with youth today is that our children do not feel genuinely loved, accepted, and cared for. With the deafening roar of disciplinarians (actually punishment-oriented) on one side and advocates of vague, difficult-to-follow programmes on the other, parents are confused.

Using designed programmes, such as those based on behaviour modification techniques, as the *primary* way of relating to your child is also a mistake. Like punishment, these programmes do have a place in child rearing and can be a very helpful, *but not as the principal way of relating to a child*. Some of these programmes are quite good, but usually their techniques are used in place of unconditional love and loving discipline (training). Here is the error. These designed techniques can be of great value in certain situations (which we will mention later), but we parents must first make sure that our child's emotional tank is as full as possible before we resort to punishment or designed techniques. In most cases, if a child receives his required amount of unconditional love and loving discipline, the parents seldom need to resort to punishment or programmes. Yes, punishment and techniques are at times necessary, quite helpful, and often good, but let's face it; they are not the best – appropriate love and guidance are.

We want the most positive, pleasant, loving relationship we can possibly have with a child. At the same time, we want him to develop self-control and act appropriately to the extent that he is able (considering his age, development, etc.). In order to see these two priceless happenings come to pass, parents must give their child two things. First, give him unconditional love, and give it appropriately. Second, give him loving discipline –

that is, training in the most positive way possible. Train by all available means, in such a way that enhances a child's self-esteem and does not demean him or hurt his self-concept. Positive guidance to good behaviour is far superior to negative punishment for poor behaviour.

But no matter how well we do our jobs as parents, a child will sometimes misbehave. This is inevitable. There are no perfect parents and there is no perfect child.

So how should we handle a child's misbehaviour? We will consider this in the next chapter.

10

Loving discipline

U p to this point we have explored how to convey unconditional love to a child by proper use of eye contact, physical contact, focused attention, and discipline (training). We have found how important it is to make sure we keep a child's emotional tank full for only then can he develop to be his best. Only then can he develop full self-control and self-discipline. We found in chapter 8 that guidance toward right action is better than punishment for wrong action. Then we ended that chapter with the fact that every child will misbehave at times. Let's now consider how to deal with misbehaviour.

In order to understand how to deal with a child's behaviour, we must understand the irrational way in which all children think. This crucial area must be carefully considered. All children need and want love. They know they need love and they know they want it, but the way in which they seek it is immature and irrational.

First, let's look at a rational way to obtain love. Say a man named Jim loved a woman named Carla. How would Jim be likely to win Carla's love? Acting immaturely, putting his worst foot forward, whining, pouting, being argumentative and demanding? Of course not. If

Jim were mature, he would be at his best. He would put his best foot forward, remain calm, pleasant, helpful, kind, and considerate. When he was not sure of Carla's love, he would not resort to immature behaviour; rather he would try to earn Carla's love. He would try to deserve it in her eyes. That's a rational way to obtain love.

But that is not the way a child does it, folks. The younger a child, the less mature he is. That makes sense, doesn't it? And the less mature he is, the more irrational he is. A child knows by nature how desperately he needs love. But he does not by nature try to deserve it or win it. This logic is beyond his inherent understanding. Eventually, he may (or may not) learn this, but he is not born with this capability.

What does a child do then, especially a younger child? A child communicates primarily with his behaviour. He continually asks the question, 'Do you love me?' How we answer that question determines many things. It determines a child's self-esteem, attitudes, feelings, peer relationships, and so on. If his emotional tank is full, you can see it in his behaviour. If it is empty, it is manifested by his behaviour. Put it this way. Most behaviour in a child is determined by how much he feels loved.

This is the irrationality of a child. Instead of winning our love and affection by good behaviour, a child by nature continually *tests* our love by his behaviour. 'Do you love me?' If we answer that all-important question, 'Yes, we love you,' great! The pressure to seek love is then off a child and his behaviour can be more easily controlled. If a child does not feel loved, by nature he is compelled more earnestly to ask, 'Do you love me?' through his behaviour. We may not like this behaviour because there are only a limited number of ways a child may act, and many of these ways may be inappropriate for the occasion. It stands to reason that when anyone is desperate enough, his behaviour may become inappropriate. Nothing makes a child more desperate than the lack of love.

This is the primary cause of misbehaviour in a child. When his emotional tank is empty, he cries out behaviourally, 'Do you love me?'

Is it fair then, or wise, to demand good behaviour from a child without first making sure he feels loved? Without first filling his emotional tank?

What does this child need?

Here's an example. When our daughter Carey was sixteen, she went to summer camp. Our nine-year-old David was then the oldest child at home, and he liked it. He acted more maturely, and sought more responsibility. David liked being the oldest. It was great.

The problem was that eventually Carey had to come home. Well, on the day she returned, David's behaviour regressed. He suddenly became whiny, discontented, pouty, somewhat angry, moody, and withdrawn.

What happened? Why the sudden, drastic change in David? What should I do as a parent? Punish David for his poor behaviour? Send Carey back to camp? Tell David his five-year-old brother Dale acts better than he? What would you do?

Well, let me explain what I did and why. Of course, Carey's coming and again becoming the oldest kid was hard on David. That's difficult for a young boy to handle. His behaviour was the pleading question, 'Do you love me? Do you love me now that Carey is home and I'm not the oldest anymore? How does your love for me compare to your love for Carey? Is she more important?

Can she take away your love from me?' Oh, the heartache of children at these times!

If I punished him at that time, how would David think I was answering his question, 'Do you love me?' As soon as I could, I took David off by himself, held him close, and we talked for some time. Occasionally I told him in boy ways how much I loved him. I gave him eye and physical contact. As his emotional tank was filled, his mood changed back to his happy, outgoing self. It took about fifteen to twenty minutes before he was off to play. David was happy and his behaviour was fine. That was one of those special moments we talked about before. I think he will never forget that precious time together. I won't.

Please don't get the idea I have been the perfect father. I have not. I've made many mistakes. But here was one situation I think I handled all right.

All this leads us to the realisation that when our child misbehaves, we must ask ourselves, 'What does this child need?'

The tendency is for parents to ask, 'What can I do to correct this child's behaviour?' Unfortunately, all too often this question leads initially to punishment. It is then difficult to consider the real needs of a child, and we may end up spanking him or sending him to his room. A child will not feel loved if we approach the handling of his misbehaviour this way.

We should always begin by asking ourselves, 'What does this child need?' Then we can proceed *logically* from there. Only then can we take care of the misbehaviour, give him what he needs, *and* permit him to feel genuinely loved.

The next step is to ask ourselves, 'Does the child need eye contact? Does he need physical contact? Does he need focused attention?' In short, does his emotional tank need filling? We parents must make sure that if the misbehaviour is in any way caused by a need for any of these, we must first meet these needs. We as parents should not continue to correct a child's behaviour until we have met his emotional needs.

This reminds me of a situation with our Dale when he was five. I had been out of town for a few days and had returned home. Dale was acting in a way which irritated me (and everyone else). He was doing all sorts of antics designed to aggravate the rest of the family, especially his nine-year-old brother, David. You see, Dale knew exactly what to do or say to make David climb the wall. And, of course, David could do the same to Dale. In fact, one son annoying the other was one of the first clues my dear wife and I had that an emotional tank needed filling.

Anyway, on this certain day, Dale was especially aggravating. He would needle his brother, pout, and make unreasonable demands. My first reaction, of course, was to really get on to him. Perhaps send him to his room; perhaps put him to bed; perhaps spank him. Then I stopped to think. 'What does he need?' The answer came in an instant. I had been out of town. He had not seen me in three days, and I had not really paid him much attention (no focused attention). No wonder Dale was asking the old question, 'Do you love me?' Actually he was asking, 'Do you still love me after being gone so long and acting as though it didn't affect me?' Suddenly his behaviour made sense. He desperately needed his daddy, and his daddy was not giving him what he needed. If I had done anything other than give him what he needed, *me*, his behaviour would have become worse. (Yes, even if I had spanked him.) He would have been deeply hurt, resentful, and I would have lost the opportunity to give him one of those special moments.

I can't tell you how thankful I am that I didn't goof on that one. I took Dale to our bedroom, held him close, and said nothing. That normally active fellow was so still and quiet against me. He just sat there and absorbed that intangible nurturing. Gradually, as his emotional tank was filled, he came to life. He began talking in his confident, easygoing, spontaneously happy way. After a short conversation about my trip, he jumped down, and ran off. Where? To find his brother, of course. When I walked into the family room, they were playing contentedly together.

So we can see how vital it is always to be asking ourselves, 'What does this child need?' If we do not, we will most assuredly skip prematurely into handling misbehaviour inappropriately. We will miss chances, to have those extremely important special moments with him. And we will punish a child at times which will hurt him in such a way that will create anger and resentment.

Fellow parents, if you miss this, you've wasted your time reading this book. Misbehaviour should not be condoned, but if it is dealt with in an inappropriate way, that is, too harshly or too permissively, you're going to have problems with that child. Yes, we must check misbehaviour. We *must* not tolerate misconduct. But the first step is *not* punishment. Punishment is occasionally necessary, but because of its negative effects from overuse, punishment should be used *only as a last resort*. It is far, far better to handle misbehaviour positively, especially with genuine love and affection, than to punish a child, especially with corporal punishment. So the first step in any situation is to make sure a child's emotional needs are met. Once again, *a child's emotional tank must be full before caring parents can take any other action.*

Is there a physical problem?

The next question to ask in the face of misbehaviour is, 'Does a physical problem exist which is precipitating this behaviour?' The younger a child, the more behaviour is affected by physical needs. Is my child hungry? Is he tired, fatigued? Is he ill? Is he coming down with something, like a cold or flu? Is he in some kind of pain or other discomfort?

This does not mean misbehaviour could be condoned if such a physical reason exists. (Misbehaviour, in my opinion, should *never* be condoned.) It means that we parents must make sure we are taking care of what is *causing* the misbehaviour as well as the misbehaviour itself. It is certainly better to correct the misbehaviour by giving a child what he needs – eye contact, physical contact, focused attention, water, food, a nap, relief of pain, or treatment of an illness – rather than punishment. Punishment may be appropriate, but we must make sure that a child has all his physical and emotional needs met first.

How can we tell when punishment is appropriate and when it will be destructive? An excellent question. It brings us to the next step in our logical way of handling misbehaviour.

Learn to forgive

In my experience, the most destructive time to punish a child for misbehaviour is when a child feels genuinely sorry for what he has done. The key word here is *genuinely*. If a child is genuinely remorseful for a wrong act, punishment (especially corporal punishment) would be harmful. The harm could come about principally in two ways.

First, if a child is already sorrowful for his inappropri-ate act, his conscience is alive and well. That's what you want! He has learned from his mistake. A good, healthy conscience is the best deterrent to repeating misbehav-iour. Punishment, especially corporal punishment, would remove the feelings of guilt and remorse and enhance the possibility for a child to forget the discom-fort of these feelings and to repeat the misconduct.

Second, punishing a child under these circumstances could provide feelings of anger. When a child already feels genuinely contrite and remorseful for his act, his con-science is dealing severely with him. He is punishing himself. He needs and is seeking comfort and reassurance that, even though his deed was bad, he is a good child. He desperately needs this assurance at such a time. So if you make the mistake of spanking him at a time when he painfully needs affection, he is deeply hurt. Under such cir-cumstances a child will then feel that he is bad as a person and that you, the parents, believe this to be true. The result is feelings of anger, hurt, resentment, and frequently bitter-ness that a child will carry with him indefinitely.

What should we parents do when a child commits a wrongful act and is genuinely sorry and remorseful about it? Scripture is a real help at this point. When we do wrong and are sorry for our wrongdoing, what does our Heavenly Father do? He forgives us. Look at this writing of the psalmist: 'Just as a father has compassion on his children, so the Lord has compassion on those who fear Him' (Psalm 103:13, NASB). With the tender-ness, compassion and forgiveness that our Heavenly Father gives to us under these circumstances, how can we then turn right around and punish *our* children?

The Apostle Paul warned of this mistake when he wrote, 'Fathers, do not exasperate your children; instead, bring them up in the training and instruction of the Lord' (Ephesians 6:4). I personally know of no surer way to provoke a child to anger, resentment, and bitterness than to punish him, especially physically, when he is genuinely sorry for his behaviour. At these times we must learn to forgive.

Another reason it is essential to forgive a child under these circumstances is that he must learn how to feel forgiven during childhood or he will have problems handling guilt. Consider how many people are guilt-laden today (including Christians) because they have never learned to feel forgiven. These poor persons may actually be truly forgiven by God and others. But they still *feel* the guilt even though they know that they are forgiven. We can save a child untold problems with guilt if we will teach him how to deal with it – namely, by the feeling of forgiveness. And we can do this by forgiving him when he is genuinely sorry for a misconduct.

A broken window

I remember an experience I had in this regard, but again please remember, just because I am picking out an example of a time when I did something right as a father doesn't mean I'm a perfect father. It just means that there are advantages to being a writer. I can pick out an example to illustrate a point.

One time I came home after a long, difficult day. I was exhausted and certainly not feeling my best. As soon as I got out of the car, David, who was nine then, ran to me. Usually David had a great big smile on his face and would jump up to give me a big bear hug. This time he was different. His face was so long and forlorn. There was a look of sadness in his beautiful blue eyes as he said, 'Dad, I have to tell you something.'

Because of my state of mind, I didn't feel I could handle a big problem very well right then. So I said, 'Let's talk about it later, OK, David?'

David looked at me very intently and replied, 'Can't we talk about it now, Dad?'

Just then I reached to open the back door of our house and noticed that one of the windows was broken. Somehow I figured out what was on David's mind.

Because I was in an irritable state of mind, I decided I had surely better handle this matter after I had relaxed. But David had followed me to my bedroom and pleaded, 'Please, let's talk about it now, Dad.'

With that pleading look on his face, what could I say? I said, 'OK, David, what would you like to talk about?' (As if I didn't know.)

David told me how he and his friends were playing ball close to the house and how a ball had hit a window and broken it. He knew he had done wrong and was obviously sorry about it. He was, through his behaviour, asking, 'Do you love me after what I did?'

So I took my son on my lap and held him dose for a little while, and said, "That's OK, David. That was an easy thing to do, and we can get the window fixed. Just play further from the house, OK?'

That was a special moment. David was immediately filled with relief. He cried briefly and just rested in my arms for a few moments. I could just feel the love flow from the child's heart. It was one of the most wonderful moments of my life. Then David was his old happy, radiant self. He jumped up and was off.

I've learned so much from this type of experience. This was one of those opportunities that do not come every day. A child does not always feel genuinely sorry for his misconduct, so we must be constantly looking for this type of opportunity to actually do what we say we should do. At these times we are able to convey to a child that, although we do not like his misconduct, we do love him no matter what. We love him unconditionally.

When a child is forgiven a misconduct, this does not mean he should not assume responsibility for its consequences. Restitution may be indicated. In the case of David's breaking the window, it may have been constructive to have had him pay for the broken glass in an appropriate way, like working it off. But again, we must make sure that the restitution is in line with the child's age, level of development, and ability to handle it.

We mustn't be manipulated. I am sure you have heard a child say, 'I'm sorry,' when he wasn't. Quite frequently a child says, 'I'm sorry' whenever he thinks he may be punished. Of course this is not being genuinely sorry or remorseful, and we must be able to distinguish the difference.

Fortunately, it is seldom difficult to tell if a child is really sorry or not. The most obvious indication is his repeating the misbehaviour. If David continued to play ball near the house after the incident, I could conclude that I had been manipulated and other measures should be taken.

If a child frequently attempts to manipulate his parents in this manner, I would be quite concerned. It could be indicative that a child's sense of right and wrong are developing in a twisted way. He could be learning to use untruthful statements to gain an advantage, saying, 'I'm sorry' simply to escape punishment. This particular behaviour is a good example of what placing the cart before the horse will develop. When parents relate to a child primarily by using punishment to control behaviour instead of first meeting a child's emotional needs, a child will develop all sorts of gimmicks to escape punishment.

One of these is 'I'm sorry' when the parents become angry or upset over a child's behaviour.

This is a dangerous situation. A child is then learning to be insincere, dishonest, calculating, manipulative, and insensitive. There is one commodity which cuts straight across this mistake and reverses the trend. It is unconditional love.

In such a situation good judgement on the part of the parents is imperative. Parents are in the best position to discern whether a child is being truthful and sincere. If a child is frequently manipulative and untruthful, trouble is ahead and help should be sought.

However, any child can do this occasionally, just as any child occasionally will feel real sorrow and guilt for misbehaviour. Wise, careful parents will realise there is a difference, discern the difference, and handle each situation appropriately.

In short, forgive a child when he is genuinely sorry, remorseful, and repentant for a misconduct. These infrequent opportunities are priceless ones and let him know beyond a doubt that you understand him, are genuinely concerned about him, and deeply love him regardless of anything else. This is unconditional love.

11

Discipline – requests, commands, rewards and punishment

What we have considered thus far are by far the most important and crucial aspects of child rearing. If these principles are applied properly, most problems of raising a child will be alleviated or averted. Meeting a child's emotional needs and applying loving discipline will permit a healthy, strong, positive lovebond between parents and their child. When any problem with a child occurs, parents must re-examine the child's needs and fill them before doing anything else.

Please remember the material in the preceding chapters because I am now going into the part of discipline which I do not like to put into print. Why? Because there are some parents who read a book such as this to glean from it only the material which they need to justify preconceived notions about child rearing. They are likely to apply only this section of the book and completely miss the fact that punishment should be used only as a last resort.

I hope you will apply the principles in the first ten chapters before trying to apply rules relating to discipline. Please love your child unconditionally and give him a superabundance of eye contact, physical contact, and focused attention. Please be careful not to love your child with possessiveness, seductiveness, vicariousness, or role-reversal. Please discipline (train) your child in *positive* ways such as guidance, example, modelling, and instruction. When your child misbehaves, ask yourself if he needs eye contact, physical contact, focused attention, rest, or water, and fill these needs first. When your child is sorry, remorseful, and repentant for a misbehaviour, please forgive him, and let him know he is forgiven.

Fellow parents, if you are diligently doing these things, and other factors such as marriage and home environment are satisfactory, things should be going fairly well with your child. Your child should be happy, responsive, well-behaved, doing what you ask him to do (according to his age and level of development) without too much difficulty. I'm not saying everything should be *perfect*, but you should be satisfied with your child, your relationship with him, and the way he is progressing.

I am saying all this now because it is a tragic mistake to expect punishment *in itself* to provide anything but negative results. Punishment without a firm foundation of unconditional love and loving discipline (training) cannot but create a poor relationship between parents and their child. Unfortunately, this is a common type of child rearing today. This is one reason children are generally having unprecedented problems today in every area, from academics to personality problems.

Requests

Proper behaviour from a child is required first by requesting it. This is the most positive way of achieving good behaviour. More importantly, requests instill a sense of personal responsibility in a child. A child feels that proper behaviour is just as much his responsibility to do as it is his parent's responsibility to see that it is done. A child knows by nature that he had a choice in how to act. When parents *request* good behaviour, a child knows his parents understand that he has ability to think and make decisions himself, has control over his behaviour, and must learn to take responsibility for it. When requests instead of commands are used as much as possible, a child will consider his parents in alliance with him in helping him to mould his own behaviour. This is so important.

If commands are primarily used in requiring proper behaviour, a child may be obedient and well behaved. But his tendency will be to act properly only because Mummy or Daddy says so, not because proper behaviour is best for him. He will not see his parents in alliance with him primarily for his own best interests. He will see them as requiring proper behaviour for the sake of good order, quietness, and their own social acceptance, in fact, for their own interests.

It is crucial to understand that making requests is a very effective way of giving instructions. It does not make us permissive or less firm. Using requests is simply a more thoughtful, pleasant, considerate way of giving instructions to a child. This is especially true when you want your child to enjoy doing things without resenting it.

For example, once when I was taking a bath, I noticed there were no towels in the bathroom. Dale, then five, was passing by, so I asked, 'Dale, would you go down and get your daddy a towel, please?' Dale was very happy to do so and was back with a towel before I could say 'Jack Robinson'.

Another example. The teacher of my son David's Sunday School class was having a problem with rowdiness from the boys. I had a choice of being very authoritarian and demanding that nine-year-old David 'behave himself, or talking over the problem with him, clarifying the issues, and then requesting his cooperation. I chose the latter, and ended the conversation with, 'I want you to pay attention to the teacher, join in the discussions, and learn all you can. Will you do that, David?' So far so good.

Direct instruction

The fact must be faced, however, that requests will not always suffice. Occasionally, parents must be forceful and give directions not by requests but by direct instruction (commands). This usually happens when a request is given to a child and he fails to carry it out. Before parents do anything else they must make sure that their request was appropriate, that it was suitable to the child's age, understanding, and ability to carry it out. The most frequent mistake in this regard is asking a child to do something which seems to be within his ability and actually is not.

A classic example of this is asking a four-year-old child to pick up his things by himself. Unless there are only two or three things to pick up, this request is unreasonable. A parent must help the child with the task. Frequently, a parent mistakenly will believe a task such as this is appropriate, gets angry when his child refuses or fails, and punishes him instead of helping him to accomplish the task.

Another real value in using requests whenever possible is to help you determine when a task is reasonable or not. You know your child better than anyone else. If on countless previous occasions your child would very willingly do a task when requested, but on one occasion he suddenly refuses, it is harmful to get angry and punish him. Obviously, because he has had no problems with this request in the past, *there is something wrong now.* Don't you want to know what it is? I believe you would. You would do your best to find the problem, because it might be extremely important. You would certainly rather take care of the problem and see your child proceed to do the task willingly than force him to do it before understanding the situation. If the reason for your child's behaviour was legitimate, then you would be the one who should be punished for forcing him to perform the task.

As a parent you have the responsibility and authority to see that your child behaves properly, but you are also responsible for your child's total welfare. You are responsible for seeing that your child is not hurt by misuse of your power and authority over him. His future happiness and welfare are heavily dependent on how you use parental authority over him.

At this point I would like to insert a very important piece of advice and warning. The more parents use such authoritative techniques as commands, scolding, nagging, or screaming, the less effective they become. It is like the boy who yelled, 'Wolf, wolf!' so many times that it lost its effect. If parents normally use pleasant requests, the occasional use of direct commands will be quite effective. The more parents use authoritative ways of telling a child what to do, the less response they will have. This is especially true if they are also angry, hostile, or hysterical when they do it.

For example, have you been in a home where the tension level is high? In these homes the parents have used essentially all their authority and reserve force just to discipline (train) their children in routine, daily events. When real forcefulness and authority are needed for unusual and really important situations, these poor parents have nothing in reserve to handle the situations. Their children then react as they usually do to their parents' wishes. They are no more responsive to emergency situations, for example, than they are to such mundane matters as tying a shoestring.

Parents, we must save the big salvos for the important situations. We must have reserve ammunition to handle critical situations. It is important to maintain pleasantness with a child by considerate, reasonable requests as much of the time as possible.

Once I made the mistake of using a forceful order when a simple request would have sufficed. The two boys and I were home, and I wanted to have the house clean before Pat came home from a weekend conference. I started out pretty well. I asked the boys to start cleaning up their bedroom while I made the beds. When I returned in a few minutes, they were busy doing their chores. But I noticed that they had thrown some clothes on the floor of their closet instead of hanging them up. David and Dale were usually obedient, easy-to-handle boys, and a short word of explanation and simple request would have sufficed. But I was somewhat annoyed and I overreacted. I barked out some orders to hang up the clothes which they were 'ruining'. See the error I made? I should not have used such forcefumess when a simple explanation and request would have been sufficient.

I should have saved forcefulness for a time when I would really need a rapid response under difficult circumstances. For example, one Sunday after we parked in our church's parking lot, Dale was walking around the car when another car pulled out. It was a dangerous situation. I yelled at Dale to run to me. Thank goodness he understood the urgency in my voice and responded immediately. If it had been my habit to yell at Dale, I know he would have responded routinely.

Another example occurred when our David and I were playing basketball with several friends. We all got carried away because we were having so much fun and we had played much too long. Consequently, we were all extremely tired. Then David fell when someone ran into him. He hurt his ankle slightly, but this pain in a very fatigued young boy was more than he could handle at that particular moment. He became angry at the person who knocked him over and began telling him about it. I saw this as inappropriate behaviour on David's part but also as a good learning experience for him.

First, I was convinced that David's emotional tank was full. He had had much affection, eye contact, physical contact, and focused attention that weekend. Second, I made a request. I asked David to go with me to a place where I could talk to him. He was too angry to respond. That is where I needed enough force to control him. The next level of use of force is to give direct instruction (command). I said, 'David, come with me,' in a firm tone. He immediately responded. When we were alone, and as he calmed down, we talked about getting so angry we lose control of our behaviour, and how to prevent it. It was a very profitable time for David because he learned much about self-control over inappropriate anger.

Suppose David simply would not have responded as I wanted him to do and could not calm down or gain control over his anger even after I commanded him to do so. The next step would have been to take him to a place where he could be by himself. If I could not get him to do this by verbal instruction, then I would have had to go to the next level of forcefulness, the use of physical force. But even here I would have used the least harsh method. I would have taken him by the hand, perhaps have one arm around his shoulder, and lead him to a quiet place. I call this 'gentle physical manipulation'. The point is to control a child's behaviour in the most gentle, most considerate, and most loving way possible.

Defiance

It is entirely possible that David could have remained unresponsive to any verbal approach. He could have refused to do as I wanted him to do in that situation. It could have developed into a battle of the wills. This could then be called *defiance*.

Defiance is openly resisting and challenging authority – parental authority. It is stubbornly refusing to obey. Of course, defiance, as well as any misbehaviour, cannot be permitted. At these times, punishment is often indicated, and such times occasionally occur no matter what we do. However, parents must attempt to avoid such unpleasant encounters – not by catering to a child's unreasonable whims or wishes, but by constantly re-examining their own expectations of their child, making sure their expectations are reasonable, considerate, and are in accordance with their child's age, level of development, and ability to respond. Yes, times which require punishment will come, but if parents find themselves punishing their child frequently, they had better re-examine their relationship with that child and what they expect from him.

But a child's defiance does not automatically mean that punishment is indicated. In fact, punishment at the wrong time can worsen the situation greatly.

Punishment, especially given often at the wrong time, can permanently harm the parent's relationship to the child. For example, if the misbehaviour is passive-aggressive in nature, punishment may cause the child to use this particular behaviour to an even greater extent as a way to upset the parent. The child's behaviour will then worsen as the child is repeatedly punished for it. Please reread the chapter 'A Child's Anger' if this is unclear to you. Misapplying punishment, especially corporal punishment during such times, can rapidly snare the parent into the 'punishment trap', where the more the child is punished, the worse the behaviour becomes.

A wise parent can avoid the punishment trap by using punishment as the last resort. A loving parent can use pleasant means of controlling a child's behaviour first with requests, explanations, and 'gentle physical manipulation'. Next the parent can use commands in a pleasant tone of voice. If unsuccessful, a parent can use a 'time out' chair where a child can sit for a reasonable length of time until he can calm down and be reasonable. These measures should be effective the vast majority of the time. However, if the parent has diligently and pleasantly tried the above ways to control a child's behaviour, then the parent can assume that the behaviour is not passive-aggressive in nature, that the punishment trap has been avoided, and punishment must now be considered.

Imagine that the child becomes obviously defiant and his defiant behaviour does not respond to filling his emotional tank, and there are no physical problems. He does not respond to requests nor to 'gentle physical manipulation', nor to explanation, nor to commands (firm instructions). He remains defiant (again, let me say this situation should be quite rare: when it occurs, make sure you have tried everything before considering punishment). He must be punished, but how?

Appropriate punishment

Determining the appropriate punishment is seldom easy. Why? The punishment must fit the offense. A child is sensitively aware of fairness and consistency. He knows when parents have overreacted or have been too harsh with him. He also knows when parents are too accepting of poor behaviour. He detects inconsistency, either with him alone or in comparison with other children, especially siblings. This is the reason parents must be firm with their child, always demanding appropriate behaviour and not being afraid to love and discipline (train) him simultaneously. But parents must remain flexible, especially regarding punishment.

Parents make mistakes. If you feel parents should not make changes in their disciplinary actions once a decision is made, you are going to back yourself into a comer. Of course, parents can change their minds, and lessen or increase the punishment. (Remember that this is a disadvantage to corporal punishment, for once done, it can't be changed.)

Naturally, parents don't want to change their minds so often that they are wishy-washy and confuse the child. For instance, if a punishment is set forth – say confinement to the bedroom for one hour, and later parents discover extenuating facts which show this punishment to be too harsh, it is logical and proper to explain this to the child and lessen the punishment. If the child has already been punished or for some other reason has suffered inappropriate punishment, it is perfectly all right for parents to apologise to the child and attempt to make the situation right.

Parents must be flexible in order to change their approach to their child when indicated. Parents must also be flexible to be able to apologise. The need occasionally to change decisions and the need to apologise occur in every home.

Being flexible in order to appropriately change our approach to handling discipline (training) and being firm are two different things. Both are essential. Firmness first of all includes what our expectations are regarding a child and his response to requests. If our expectations are too rigid (for example, expecting a two-year-old to consistently respond to first requests), we are being unreasonable. A normal two-year-old will naturally be negative most of the time and seem to be quite disobedient and defiant. But this is a normal stage of development – let's call it 'two-year-old negativism'. Punishment for this is unwarranted. Loving parents of a two-year-old will, of course, be firm, but firm in *limit setting*, not in punishment. These parents will control the child's behaviour by gently manoeuvring the child physically, for example, picking him up, turning him around, guiding him, or placing him in the correct place or position – 'gentle physical manipulation'.

This 'two-year-old negativism' is crucial for normal child development. The child will eventually do what we ask but he must say 'no' first. This is one of the ways each of us had to separate ourselves psychologically from our parents. It may appear to be defiance but it is distinctively different. One difference between two-year-old negativism and defiance is belligerence. Two-year-old negativism is normal and should not be punished. Belligerent defiance on the other hand cannot be tolerated and must be dealt with quickly. Incidentally, 'two-year-old negativism' can occur in any age child.

As a child becomes older, his ability to respond to verbal requests increases, and by the time he reaches four and one-half (this varies from child to child), parents can expect him to respond to first requests. I fully expected my children to respond to first requests. If they did not, they knew that action would be taken. Of course they were free to make an appropriate statement regarding the request, if they had any question about it. But unless I changed the request, they knew they must carry it out.

It is so important to remember that being firm does not mean being unpleasant. We must be firm in our expectations and enforcement of these expectations, but we will be just as effective by doing it pleasantly. Loving firmness does not require us to be angry, loud, authoritative, or otherwise unpleasant.

Every child needs to experience all the ways of loving simultaneously. He needs eye contact, physical contact, focused attention, *and* discipline *simultaneously*. A child must have a parent's love and firmness together. None of these things are mutually exclusive. Being firm does not negate affection. Showing affection does not lessen firmness or foster permissiveness. *Lack of firmness and limit setting foster permissiveness, but love and affection do not.*

When parents have conscientiously provided all of the preceding means of loving and disciplining a child, and the youngster remains belligerently defiant, the parents must punish him. This type of defiance must be broken. The punishment must be severe enough to break the belligerent defiance, but it must also be as mild as possible to prevent the problems we have already discussed. If a command or explanation to a child is sufficient to break the defiance, why be more punitive? If sending a child to his room for a period is required and will suffice, fine. If taking a privilege away from a child is necessary to crush the defiance, proceed to do so. Let's face it, corporal punishment is sometimes necessary to break a pronounced belligerent defiance, but only as a last resort.

Another problem with punishment is that punishment for one child may mean little to another. For example, one of my boys was more sensitive than the other. The most severe punishment for him was to send him to his room. This rejection was far more devastating to him than corporal punishment. Yet, my other boy didn't mind going to his room at all. Each child is unique.

One other problem with punishment is that the type and severity of punishment usually depends on the parent's feelings at the time. At times when the parent is in a pleasant, upbeat, loving mood, the punishment will most likely be quite different and less harsh than when the parent is in a negative mood. This, of course, leads to inconsistent discipline which has its own unhealthy effects on the child. For these reasons, I suggest that parents confer with each other or with a friend and determine appropriate punishment for each child in each situation. This decision-making should be done, of course, when the parent is calm, rational, and is able to think the matter completely through.

Be careful

When physical punishment is used, we must be careful in several respects. First, the child must understand exactly why he is being punished. Explain to him in terms of his behaviour exactly what he has done wrong. Words such as 'bad boy' or 'bad girl' can hurt the child's self-esteem and should not be used.

Second, parents must be careful not to inflict any physical damage on the child. For example, it is easy to hurt a finger or another part of the body inadvertently.

Third, immediately after the punishment, as the child is crying, he should be left alone. Parents should stay nearby, however, listening for the crying to stop. When a child's crying has subsided and he is looking around, a child is again asking, 'Do you love me? Do you still love me?' Parents should then give the child an abundance of eye contact, physical contact, and focused attention to reassure him that he is indeed loved.

Behaviour modification

Finally, I believe it appropriate to mention *behaviour modification*. This is a system of thought which is in wide use today concerning the handling of children. Behaviour modification utilises positive reinforcement (interjecting a positive commodity into a child's environment), negative reinforcement (withdrawing a positive commodity from a child's environment), and punishment (interjecting a negative commodity into a child's environment). An example of positive reinforcement is rewarding a child for an appropriate behaviour by giving him some sweets or fruit. An example of negative reinforcement is withdrawing television privileges from a child for inappropriate behaviour. An example of punishment (sometimes called aversive technique) is pinching him on the trapezius muscle for inappropriate behaviour.

It is beyond the scope of this book to speak on this subject in depth. However, a few important points should be made.

First of all, such emphasis has been made concerning behaviour modification that such techniques are frequently substituted for emotional nurturing. If behaviour modification is overused by parents in relation to a child, a child will not feel loved. Why? First of all, the very foundation of behaviour modification is *conditional*. A child receives a reward only if he *behaves* a certain way.

Second, behaviour modification is not concerned with feelings or the emotional needs of a child (love). Consequently, parents, using behaviour modification as the primary way of relating to your child, cannot convey unconditional love.

For instance, consider the example I used in the last chapter regarding filling Dale's emotional tank when he misbehaved following my three-day absence. A strict behaviourist would say I was rewarding Dale for his misbehaving by giving him affection at that time. See the difference? Parents cannot *primarily* use behaviour modification in relating to their child and love their child unconditionally.

Another problem with relating to a child primarily by behaviour modification is that a child will derive an inappropriate value system. He will learn to do things primarily for a reward. A 'what's-in-it-for-me?' orientation will develop. An example of this occurred at the home of a dear friend of ours. He happens to be a strict behaviourist and was raising his children as closely to the behaviour modification concept as he could. One evening, when we were eating at their home, he said, 'Jerry is just three and he can count to a hundred already. Watch this.' He went up to his son and said, 'Jerry, count to a hundred and I'll give you some sweets.' Jerry instantly replied, 'I don't want any sweets.' If we want our child to do things for the satisfaction of doing them or for the pride of a job well done, we should not behaviour modification. The end result is inappropriate motivation.

One other problem with the use of behaviour modification is this. If parents overuse these techniques, a child will learn to gain what he wants by using the same method on the parents. He will behave as the parents wish *in order to get something he wants*. Most persons would call this manipulation. One of the surest ways of encouraging your child to become cunning and manipulative is to use behaviour modification techniques too often.

Now that I've expounded on the negative aspects of behaviour modification, let me express the positive. There is a place for these techniques in child rearing, but not as the primary way of relating to a child (the primary way must be unconditional love).

Behaviour modification should be used for specific, recurring behavioural problems for which a child is neither sorry nor defiant. This type of problem must also be specific enough to be easily defined and understood by a child.

Here is an example of this type of problem which we encountered in our home. When our two boys were nine and five years of age, they were at stages during which they frequently fought with each other. Of course, neither one was remorseful about this. Forgiveness was certainly inappropriate. And neither one was defiant about it. Requests did not work. Commands had effect only for a few hours. Punishments also had brief effects and were quite unpleasant for everyone. You know what worked? You've probably guessed it, a reward system.

We used a chart-with-stars technique. One star for every fifteen minutes of peace, gradually increasing the time interval until the fighting was extinguished. We gave each boy an appropriate reward for a certain number of stars. It worked beautifully and we had 'peace in the valley'.

However, one word of warning about this type of technique. It takes time, consistency, real effort, and persistence. Don't start something like this unless you are prepared to stick with it and be consistent. Otherwise it will fail.

There are numerous good books on behaviour modification to tell you more about specific techniques.

This has been a long chapter, but one more point. As you can tell, good child rearing requires balance. A child needs everything we have discussed; eye contact, physical contact, focused attention, discipline, requests, firmness, flexibility, commands, forgiveness, punishment, behaviour modification, instruction, guidance, example, and active listening. But we must give our children these things in *proper measure*. May our discussions help you to do this in a way that will enable your child to feel unconditionally loved.

12

Children with special problems

Why do children with special problems such as diabetes, learning disabilities, deafness, hyper-activity, or mental retardation generally have markedly greater emotional and behavioural problems? The answer to this question is extremely complex. To explain why children in each of these problem areas are more prone to emotional and behavioural disturbance is more than can be dealt with in this book.

However, a few very pertinent points would be helpful to every parent of such a child. Some of these facts are closely related to conveying love to our children.

Perceptual problems

First, let's look at the general area of perceptual problems. To perceive is difficult to define, but let's try. It can mean to grasp or take in information through the senses to the mind, in which case a child with perceptual problems has difficulty taking in information from his environment and transmitting it to his mind. Consequently, when such information as visual images, sound, and touch is processed in a child's mind, he has difficulty understanding it clearly. His understanding of his environment is distorted in those areas where his misperceptions lie.

Using this very broad and simplified definition of perceptual problems, we can see that many special problems can be included. Visual problems, hearing problems, certain neurological diseases, and many type of learning disabilities have one thing in common: each child suffering from one of these disorders has a distorted conception of his surroundings. In one or more ways his incoming stimuli or information are distorted to him.

Do you see the great significance of this beyond the perceptual disability *per se*? Every way you have to convey your love to your child requires the use of one or more of the perceptual senses? Eye contact requires the perceiving of visual imagery. Physical contact requires the use of the sense of touch, which in itself is overwhelmingly complex. Focused attention requires the use of all of your senses. So if there is enough perceptual distortion in any of these areas, your child's understanding of how you feel about him can be distorted. This makes it more difficult to convey your love to this particular child.

This difficulty in a child's feeling loved is one big reason perceptually handicapped children generally have less than adequate self-concepts. It is one reason they usually become increasingly depressed as they grow older, frequently resulting in rather severe emotional and behavioural disorders, especially in early adolescence.

The common story of a perceptually handicapped child with resultant learning disabilities is that this unfortunate child cannot keep up academically or in other ways with his peers. He makes poor grades or is in other ways forced to endure continual degrading experiences. Even in nongraded situations he realises his deficiencies. As he goes into the pre- and early adolescent years, he becomes increasingly depressed. Depression in this age group is unlike any other. Generally these children do not look or act depressed unless the depression has reached severe depths. Typically young teenagers manifest their depression by difficulty in paying attention in the classroom (decreased attention span and ability to concentrate) with a resultant dropping of grades. Subsequently, prolonged boredom sets in with decreased interest in wholesome activities. At this stage the youngster is profoundly miserable.

If the boredom continues, eventually the teenager will act out his depression and misery. A severely depressed and bored girl in this predicament may then become promiscuous, use drugs, run away, or may try other antisocial behaviours. A boy in a comparable situation will be prone to behave similarly but is usually more inclined to such actions as stealing and fighting.

If we know that perceptually handicapped children are almost predisposed to poor self-concept feelings of being unloved and unacceptable, and of depression, how can we help them? I firmly believe that the area where they require the greatest help is the area which is largely over-looked. You guessed it, these children need most of all to feel genuinely, unconditionally loved. They will then be better able to overcome their handicaps.

How do we do this? The same way we give our love to all children, except that we must remember that, though their perceptions are distorted in some areas, they are seldom distorted in all sensual modalities. These children almost always need more affection and other means of conveying love in order to feel loved. In addition, they need our love to be given to them in more direct, simplified, straightforward, and accentuated ways. We must also give it to them in a somewhat more intense manner. All of this is necessary to make sure that these children do not misunderstand our feeling toward them. Our love-communications with such children must be clear and strong.

Other medical problems

Children with chronic (long standing) medical problems are also prone to emotional and behavioural problems. This is especially true of medical problems which require close supervision and continual attention such as juvenile diabetes. Taking care of young children with this disease requires tremendous time and effort by parents. So much so that it is difficult not to devote one's full attention to treating the disease and overlooking other needs of the children. This is exactly what happens concerning the emotional needs of most of these children. The caring parents become so intent, for example, on giving the right doses of insulin, regulating the diet, doing glucose determinations and the like, that these necessary procedures replace the natural giving of love. As essential as they are, these medical duties are no substitute for unconditional love given through eye contact, physical contact, and focused attention. As children grow older, especially during adolescence, they become increasingly angry, resentful, and bitter about their disease. Because of the aforementioned substitution of medical care for love, the children resent the disease and their parents. They become hostile and defiant not only toward parental authority but all authority. They are inclined to depression and all of its consequences. Worst of all, they frequently use the seriousness of their illness to defy parents and express anger and frustration. This may be done by taking too much insulin, eating too many carbohydrates, and so on. Some actually kill themselves as an angry defiant act.

Of course, there are other reasons in this complex illness which contribute to young patients' bitter and destructive attitudes. In my experience, however, there are two principal reasons why these unfortunate children become so intensely resentful and defiant. The first is as we just discussed, substitution of medical procedures as a manifestation of love. The other is poor limit-setting and lack of behavioural control by the parents. The parents may feel pity for the children in their illness. They may also feel guilt, fear, or depression. If the parents cannot control the children's behaviour in the same manner as they would other children, namely with firmness, the children will be able to manipulate the parents. This is especially easy for chronically ill children to do. They can use their illness to control their parents by taking advantage of the parents' guilt and pity, by making the parents fearful that the children's condition may worsen, and even by using the outright threat of purposely succumbing to the illness.

These dynamics may occur to some extent with any children with a prolonged disability, illness, or other problem. Examples include asthma, chronic bronchitis, heart defects, physical deformity, mental retardation, seizure disorders, neurological diseases, muscular diseases, dental problems, and even learning disabilities. The list goes on and on.

So, dear parents, if your child has a handicap, a problem of any kind, do not become so wrapped up with the problem that you neglect the child. He needs your unconditional love far more than anything else. Far more than braces, far more than tutoring or other academic remediation, far more than any exercise, and far more than any medicine. The most indispensable ingredients in your child's life are you and your giving unconditional love to him. With that, your child can derive the strength and will to overcome and develop.

The resistant child

Now, let's consider help for the resistant child, namely, one who is resistant to receiving affection. Yes, believe it or not, many children are naturally (congenitally) resistant to the natural ways of giving affection and love. They resist eye contact, they do not want to be touched, and they do not care for focused attention.

This may occur in varying degrees. Some children are only mildly resistant whereas others are quite uncomfortable with the conveying of love. Some children may be comfortable with one way of conveying love but not another. Each child is unique.

The resistant child is invariably an enigma to his parents. Caring parents instinctively know that their child needs affection and other forms of emotional nurturing; but when they try to meet this need, the child finds innumerable ways to avoid receiving love. What a dilemma. Many parents eventually resign themselves to what they conclude is 'what the child wants'. They assume that the child does not need their attention, love, and affection. This is a disastrous mistake.

Even the extremely resistant child needs everything we have talked about concerning unconditional love. However, since he is uncomfortable accepting it, we parents must gradually teach this child to receive love comfortably.

We can begin by understanding the five periods during which a child is able to receive love. During these periods the child's defenses are down, and he is able to relate closely enough on the emotional level to be receptive. Of course, every child is different. One child may be more receptive during one period and less receptive during another. It behoves parents to know when their child is most receptive to love and affection.

The first receptive period is when a child finds something to be quite humorous. For instance, a child may be watching television and see a funny scene. At this time parents have the opportunity to make eye contact, physical contact, and focused attention while commenting on the humorous subject. Parents must usually be quick in doing this because the defenses of a truly resistant child are down only briefly. We've got to 'get in and get out' or a child may defend against similar tactics in the future.

The second period of receptivity is when a child has accomplished something for which he is justifiably proud. It cannot be just anything. The accomplishment must be something a child feels genuinely good about. At these times, parents can make eye and physical contact (and focused attention if appropriate) while praising a child. Again, we must be careful not to overdo it, especially by prolonging it; again 'get in and get out'.

The third receptive period is at such times when a child is not well physically. A child may be ill or hurt, and his receptivity at these times is somewhat unpredictable. Sometimes illness or pain may increase a child's ability to receive affection, but at other times a child's resistance may increase. We parents should continually monitor this in order to take advantage of opportunities to give love at these times of illness or pain. A child will never forget special moments such as these.

The fourth period of receptivity occurs when a child is hurt emotionally. This frequently happens when he has a conflict with peers and the peers have taken unfair advantage of him. At these times of emotional pain, many resistant children become able to accept our showing love to them.

The fifth receptive period largely depends upon previous experiences of a particular child. For example, one child may have had many pleasant, meaningful experiences while going on long walks with his parents. Such a child will quite likely be more receptive to parental conveying of love while on walks. Another child may have had pleasant experiences at bedtime when his parents would read, pray, and talk with him. He will naturally be inclined to be more receptive at bedtime. This is why providing routine times of pleasant, warm experiences for a child is very important and pays large dividends to child and parents. Bedtime routine, for example, is a good investment.

In a nutshell, all children need the natural ways of conveying love – eye contact, physical contact, and focused attention. If a child is not receiving an ample amount, we should find out why and correct the situation.

13

Helping your child spiritually

O ne of the chief complaints we hear from teenagers today is the failure of their parents to give them ethical or moral standards to live by in formative years. This yearning is expressed by older children in many ways. One adolescent says he needs 'meaning in life'. Another wants a 'standard to guide her'. Other seeking youngsters long for 'something to hold on to' or 'someone to show me how to live'.

These desperate cries do not come from a few unhappy, discontented teenagers. Most adolescents are feeling and expressing these yearnings. They are confused – terribly confused – in this existential area of living. It is quite unusual to find young people who have 'got it together' in regard to a meaning and purpose in this life, who are at peace with themselves and their world, and who have perspective and understanding about living in this confused, changing, fearful world today. And much goes back to their childhood.

A child first looks to his parents for direction that enables him to develop healthy values. Whether he finds what he needs from his parents depends on two things. The first is whether the parents have it themselves. The second is whether a child can identify with his parents in such a way as to incorporate and accept parental values. A child who does not feel loved will find this difficult.

The first requirement

Let's look at the first requirement that is necessary in giving a child that longed-for meaning to life. We parents must possess a foundation upon which to base our lives and which can withstand the test of time – something that will support us through every phase of living: adolescence, young adulthood, middle age, old age, marriage crises, financial crises, children's crises, energy crises, and especially, a rapidly changing society in which spiritual values are swiftly eroding. We parents must have that crucial foundation upon which we base our lives in order to give it to our child. In my opinion, it is the most valuable treasure we can pass on to our offspring.

What is this indispensable possession which gives purpose and meaning to life and is transferable to our child? Many have sought after it since the beginning of civilisation but few have really found it. Philosophers have been struggling with these questions and answers for centuries. International diplomats have occasionally claimed some answers. Government planners are claiming to have answers even now, and their diligently planned legislation will leave hearts just as empty and longing as before, but more dependent upon man's (government's) control. The field of mental health offers help concerning emotional problems, mental disturbances, psychophysiological disorders, adaptational problems, and marital disharmony.

But this treasurable, peace-giving possession which every heart craves is God Himself. He is intimately personal, yet can be shared with another. He is strengthening in times of conflict, yet is comforting in times of distress. He gives wisdom in times of confusion, yet gives correction in times of error. He provides help in times past and present, yet promises even more in the future. He gives direction and guidance at all times, yet does not send us out alone – He stays closer than a brother.

He gives directions to be carried out, yet gives amazingly wonderful promises to those who are willing to obey. He allows loss and pain at times, but He always heals and replaces the loss with something better. He does not force Himself upon us, but patiently waits to be accepted. He does not coerce us into doing His will, but is deeply distressed and hurt when we follow the wrong path. He wants us to love Him because He first loved us, but He gave us a free will to choose Him or reject Him. He wants to take care of us, but refuses to force Himself upon us. His greatest desire is to be our Father, but He will not intrude. If we want what He wants, a loving, caring, Father-child relationship with Him – we must accept His offer. He is too considerate to force it. He is waiting for you and me to open our lives to Him and become His children. Of course, as you have guessed. He must be a personal God.

This personal, intimate relationship with God through His Son Jesus Christ is the most important thing in life. This is the 'something' which our young people are yearning for: the 'meaning in life,' 'something to count on,' 'higher guidance,' 'something to bring comfort when everything seems to be falling apart.' It is all there.

Do you have it? If you do not, seek help from a minister or Christian friend; or write me through the publisher, and I will send you helpful material.

The second requirement

The second requirement necessary in order to give a child what we have is that a child identify with his parents so as to accept and incorporate the parents' values.

As you recall, if a child does not feel loved and accepted, he has real difficulty identifying with his parents and their values. Without a strong, healthy love-bond with his parents, a child reacts to parental guidance with anger, resentment, and hostility. He views each parental request (or command) as an imposition and learns to resist it. In severe cases, a child learns to consider each parental request with such resentment that his total orientation to parental authority (and eventually to all authority, including God's) is doing the opposite of what is expected of him.

With this type of attitude and orientation, you can see how difficult it becomes to give your child your moral and ethical value system.

In order for a child to identify with his parents (relate closely with them) and be able to accept their standards, he must feel genuinely loved and accepted by them. To give a child the close relationship with God which they possess, parents must make sure that a child feels unconditionally loved. Why? Because this is the way God loves us – unconditionally. It is extremely difficult for persons who do not feel unconditionally loved by their parents to feel loved by God. This is the greatest and most common obstacle to many people in establishing a personal relationship with God. Parents must prevent this from happening to their own children.

How do parents ensure that their child is prepared and ready to accept God's love? By ensuring that they fill his emotional needs and keep his emotional tank full. Parents cannot expect a child to find a close, warm, *rewarding* relationship with God unless they have cared for him emotionally and he has such a relationship with them.

Yes, I have seen children who were raised by corporal punishment become Christians. But because they were raised primarily by inflicting physical pain instead of unconditional love, these unfortunate people seldom have a healthy, loving, warm relationship with God. They tend to use their religion punitively against others under the guise of 'helping' them. They use biblical command-ments and other scriptural statements to justify their own harsh, unloving behaviour. They also tend to set them-selves up as spiritual magistrates dictating the propriety of others. It is possible, of course, for any child eventu-ally to find his way into God's loving arms and to accept His love. With God anything is possible. Unfortunately, a child's chances are markedly diminished if his parents have not given him a loving foundation.

So there are two requirements essential to helping a child spiritually: A parent's personal relationship with God, and a child's assurance that he is unconditionally loved.

A child's memory

The next important thing to know about a child is how his memory operates. Remember that a child is much more emotional than cognitive. He therefore remembers feelings much more readily than facts. A child can remember how he felt in a particular situation much eas-ier than he can remember the details of what went on.

Let me give you a very pertinent example. A child in a Sunday School class will remember exactly how he felt long after he forgets what was said or taught.

So, in some ways, whether a child's experience was pleasant or unpleasant is much more important than the details of what a teacher taught. By pleasant, I do not mean that a teacher need cater to a child's desire for fun and frolic. I mean treating a child with respect, kindness, and concern. Make him feel good about himself. Do not criticise, humiliate, or otherwise put him down. Naturally, what a child is taught is extremely important, but if it is a degrading or boring experience for a child, he is very likely to reject even the very best teaching, especially if morality and ethics are involved. It is from this type of situation that a child develops a bias against religious matters, and tends to consider church people as hypocrites. This attitude is difficult to rectify and can continue with him for a lifetime. On the other hand, if the teaming experience is a pleasant one, a child's memories of spiritual teaching will be pleasant and can then be incorporated into a child's own personality.

As an illustration, friends of ours had an eight-year-old son, Michael, who used to enjoy Sunday School and being taught about spiritual things. There was no problem getting him to go to the Lord's house. Sadly, one Sunday morning, Michael and another energetic boy were talking and laughing during a presentation by the teacher. In anger, the teacher put Michael and his friend in a small room by themselves and made them write 'Thou shalt honour thy mother and thy father' over and over until Michael's parents came to get him. The unreasonableness and insensitiveness of that unjust and humiliating punishment had dramatic effects. It induced such anger, hurt, and resentment that Michael began holding animosity toward anything spiritual. He didn't want to return to his church, and, of course, his conception of God was severely damaged. Only after several months were his loving parents able to help Michael again trust spiritual truths. This type of thing, in greater or lesser extremes, happens when the importance of a teacher's teaching is placed before the emotional welfare of a child. Emotionality and spirituality are not entirely separate entities. One is quite related to and dependent upon the other. For this reason, if parents want to help a child spiritually, they must care for him first emotionally. Because a child remembers feelings much more easily than facts, there must be a series of pleasant memories upon which to accumulate the facts, especially spiritual facts.

A popular misconception

At this point, let's examine a popular misconception. It goes something like this: 'I want my child to learn to make his own decisions after he is exposed to everything. He shouldn't feel he has to believe what I believe. I want him to learn about different religions and philosophies; then when he has grown up he can make his own decision.'

This parent is copping out or else is grossly ignorant of the world we live in. A child brought up in this manner is indeed one to be pitied. Without continual guidance and clarification in ethical, moral, and spiritual matters, he will become increasingly confused about his world. There are reasonable answers to many of life's conflicts and seeming contradictions. One of the finest gifts parents can give a child is a clear, basic understanding of the world and its confusing problems. Without this stable base of knowledge and understanding, is it any wonder many children cry to their parents, 'Why didn't you give me a meaning for all this? What's it all about?'

Another reason this approach to spirituality is grossly negligent is this. More and more groups, organisations, and cults are offering destructive, enslaving, and false answers to life's questions. These people would like nothing more than to find a person who was brought up in this seemingly broad-minded way. He is easy prey for any group offering concrete answers, no matter how false or enslaving.

It is amazing to me how some parents can spend thousands of dollars and go to any length of political manipulation to make sure their child is well prepared educationally. Yet, for the most important preparation of all, for life's spiritual battles and finding real meaning in life, a child is left to fend for himself and made easy prey for cultists.

Every child loves a story

How do parents prepare their children spiritually? Organised religious instruction and activities are extremely important to a developing child. However, nothing influences a child more than his home and what he is exposed to there. This holds true regarding spiritual things as well. Parents must be actively involved in a child's spiritual growth. They cannot afford to leave it to others, even superb church youth workers.

First, parents themselves must teach their children spiritual concerns. They must teach not only spiritual facts, but how to apply them in everyday life. This is not easy.

It is quite simple to give a child basic scriptural facts such as who different Bible persons were and what they did. But that is not what we are ultimately after. A child needs to understand what meaning biblical characters and principles have for him personally. We can only teach this at somewhat of a sacrifice to ourselves, as with focused attention. We must give focused attention and be willing to spend time alone with a child in order to provide for his emotional needs as well as his spiritual. In fact, whenever possible, why not do them simultaneously?

Bedtime is usually the best time to accomplish this, for most children are then eager to interact with their parents. Whether it is because their emotional tanks need filling or because they want to delay bedtime makes little difference. The point is that it is a great opportunity to meet the emotional needs of a child, give him spiritual training and guidance, and do it in an atmosphere which a child will remember fondly. By what other means can parents give so much to a child in such an economical way?

Every child loves a story. When our children were growing up, Pat and I would often read to an individual child, sometimes a secular story, at other times a story from a Christian book. I even got requests for stories that I made up – 'Bing Bing and Bong Bong', 'The Great Rutabaga', and other fanciful tales.

We also made it a point to read short devotional stories. My boys especially loved to answer questions about the stories, and books with questions after each story were good for our purpose. Most of the books we used when our children were young are likely out of print, but a visit to a Christian bookstore will acquaint you with many good books you can use with your children.

As a child answers questions following the reading of a story, there are always similarities and applications to what is going on in his own life. The hard part is getting the message across to a child and, because many parents feel awkward and inept at this, they usually give it up, especially if a child doesn't contribute much. Don't let these things stop you! Whether a child appears to be responding or not, you can rest assured that you are strongly influencing him. Your time spent with your child in this way will have far reaching effects. If you don't influence your child in the area of the supernatural now, someone else will do it later.

Share your spiritual life

One more point about helping a child spiritually. With the factual knowledge gained from church, Sunday School, and home, a child only has the raw materials with which to grow in his spiritual life. He must learn to use this knowledge effectively and accurately to become a mature person spiritually. To do this, a child must have the experience of walking with God daily and learning to rely on Him personally.

The best way to help a child with this is to share your own spiritual life with him. Of course, this depends on the quality of what you have to share, and how much you share depends on the child, his age, level of development, and ability to comprehend and handle it.

As a child matures, we parents want to gradually increase sharing with him how we ourselves love God, walk daily with Him, rely on Him, seek His guidance and help, thank Him for His love, care, gifts, and answered prayer.

We want to share these things with our child *as they happen*, not afterward. Only in that way can a child get on-the-job training. Sharing past experiences is simply giving additional factual information, not letting a child learn for himself through his own experience. There is a lot of truth in the old statement, 'Experience is the best teacher.' Let him share in yours. The sooner a child learns to trust God, the stronger he will become.

A child needs to learn how God meets all personal and family needs, including financial. He needs to know what his parents are praying for. For example, he needs to know when you are praying for the needs of others. He should (again, as appropriate) know of problems for which you are asking God's help. And don't forget to keep him informed about how God is working in your life, how He is using you to minister to someone. And, of course, a child should certainly know you are praying for him and for his individual, particular needs.

Finally, a child must be taught by example how to forgive and how to find forgiveness both from God and people. Parents do this first of all by forgiving. Next, when they make a mistake, they apologise and ask for God's forgiveness. I cannot overstress how important that is. So many people today have problems with guilt. They cannot forgive and/or they cannot feel forgiven. What can be more miserable? But the fortunate person who has learned how to forgive those who offend him and is able to ask and receive forgiveness, demonstrates a mark of mental health and finds peace as a result.

As we end our discussion, I hope you will seriously consider the principles stressed in this book. It was written especially for you by a parent who himself has learned by experience at home and in his profession that parents must truly love their children to see them grow into strong, healthy, happy, and independent adults. Now, perhaps you will want to go back and reread this volume and underline principles that you determine to put into practice as you seek to really love your child. I challenge you to do so.